The Purpose of My Life as a Woman

The Purpose of My Life as a Woman

Diane Mellenger

THE PURPOSE OF MY LIFE AS A WOMAN
By: Diane Mellenger
Copyright © 2011
GOSPEL FOLIO PRESS

Published by
GOSPEL FOLIO PRESS
304 Killaly St. W.
Port Colborne, ON L3K 6A6
CANADA

ISBN:9781926765549

Cover design by Danielle Elzinga

All Scripture quotations from the
King James Version unless otherwise noted.

Printed in USA

The Purpose of My Life

The purpose of your life is to learn to live in accord with who you are by Creation.

> *"And God said, 'Let Us make man in our image, after Our likeness: and let them have dominion over the fish of the sea, and over the fowl of the air, and over the cattle and over all the earth, and over every creeping thing that creeps upon the earth.'*
>
> *"And God blessed them, and God said unto them 'Be fruitful, and multiply, and replenish the earth, and subdue it…'"* (Gen. 1:6,7).

Your soul was created in the image of God and your task is to devote your life to making choices that authenticate your God-given self. When you make significant contributions and enjoy rewarding accomplishments based on who you are, and on who God made you, you will have a life of fulfilled purpose.

The Purpose of My Life

The purpose of your life is to...

> *"Fear God and keep His commandments; for this is the whole duty of man"* (Eccl. 12:13).

This is the true way for true happiness. We are to reverence Him, to claim His authority and dread His terrible wrath. To fear God is to worship Him and give Him honour and true devotion.

> *"Jesus said unto him, 'Thou shalt love the Lord thy God with all thy heart, and with all thy soul, and with all thy mind. This is the first and great commandment'"* (Matt. 22:37, 38).

The Purpose of My Life

We are to have fellowship with God.

"God is faithful, by whom you were called unto the fellow-ship of His Son Jesus Christ our Lord" (1 Cor. 1:9).

God is faithful and we are to have fellowship with Him. He has brought us into a relationship with His Son and when we believe on His Son we will have an inheritance in Christ.

January 4

The Purpose of My Life

Your life purpose is to be conformed to the image of Christ.

"For whom He did foreknow, He also did predestinate to be conformed to the image of His Son, that He might be the firstborn among many brethren" (Rom. 8:29).

We are to walk like Christ, to live like Christ, and to bear our suffering like the Lord Jesus Christ. We are to be separated unto God and when we give ourselves to Christ, God gives us to Him (Christ); and in giving us to Him, He predestinated us to be conformed to His image.

The Purpose of My Life

We are created for His pleasure.

"Thou are worthy, O Lord, to receive glory and honour and power: for Thou hast created all things, and for Thy pleasure they are and were created" (Rev. 4:11).

It was God's pleasure to create all things. God does not delight in the death of sinners, but He wishes that all men would repent.

"For by Him were all things created, that are in heaven, and that are in earth, visible and invisible, whether they be thrones, or dominions, or principalities, or powers: all things were created by Him, and for Him" (Col. 1:16).

January 6

The Purpose of My Life

We are to know God.

"Grace and peace be multiplied unto you through the knowledge of God, and of Jesus our Lord" (2 Pet. 1:2).

Knowledge of God and having faith in Him is our source of spiritual support and comfort. We must acknowledge God as the author of our salvation wherein we find grace and peace in our Lord Jesus Christ.

The Purpose of My Life

We are to become like the Lord and to be filled with the fullness of Christ.

> *"Till we all come in the unity of the faith, and of the knowledge of the Son of God, unto a perfect man, unto the measure of the stature of the fullness of Christ"* (Eph. 4:13).

When we become God's children, through faith in the Lord Jesus Christ, He expects us to grow and mature and to be like Christ.

January 8

The Purpose of My Life

There are many words in the Bible which God has written to bring men and women to a knowledge of Himself. For example:

"Trust in the Lord with all thine heart; and lean not unto thine own understanding" (Prov. 3:5).

By faith (from the heart) we must put our trust in the Lord Jesus Christ if we want to go to Heaven and be with Him forever.

The Purpose of My Life

The word *"believe"* is what God uses to explain His salvation for mankind.

> *"For God so loved the world that he gave his only begotten Son, that whosoever believes in him should not perish, but have everlasting life"* (John 3:16).

or

> *"Believe on the Lord Jesus Christ, and thou shalt be saved"* (Act 16:31).

You can be saved from a hopeless life and saved from hell. In order to redeem sinful mankind, God loved the world and sent His only son, Jesus Christ.

January 10

The Purpose of My Life

God also uses the word *"saved."* In God's eyes you are either saved or lost. You are either going to Heaven or Hell.

> *"For by grace are you saved through faith, and that not of yourselves: it is the gift of God; not of works, lest any man should boast"* (Eph. 2:8).

It is God's grace that gets us to Heaven when we accept Jesus Christ as our own personal Lord and Saviour. We cannot get to heaven on our own beliefs or good works. Salvation is a gift and we must believe in the Lord Jesus Christ to receive it.

The Purpose of My Life

In John 3:3, Jesus answered Nicodemus, a ruler of the Jews; *"Verily, verily, I say unto you, Except a man be born again, he cannot see the kingdom of God."*

First of all you are born into your earthly family. But in order to get into God's family you must be born again. This is a spiritual birth. It is not good enough to have always believed in Jesus; there should be a time and place when you repented of your sin and believed on the Lord Jesus Christ as your Saviour and Lord, for time and eternity.

The Purpose of My Life

God expects us to *"repent."* We need to repent because all are guilty in God's sight and God cannot look on evil. He hates sin and sin cannot enter Heaven or it would not be Heaven any more. Jesus preached,

> *"I tell you, Nay: but, except you repent, you shall all likewise perish"* (Luke 13:3).

Repentance becomes before believing.

> *"The time is fulfilled, and the kingdom of God is at hand: repent ye, and believe the gospel"* (Mark 1:15).

The Purpose of My Life

"Converted" is a word that God uses.

"Repent ye therefore, and be converted, that your sins my be blotted out..." (Acts 3:19).

You are to turn from your sins and to turn to Christ as your Lord and Saviour and He will save you.

There are people who want the benefits of being identified with the Lord Jesus without turning away from sin.

The Purpose of My Life

Faith is the fundamental teacher of God.

> *"But without faith it is impossible to please Him; for He that comes to God must believe that He is, and that He is a rewarder of them that diligently seek Him"* (Heb. 11:6).

Faith is necessary for salvation. When we sit down on a chair we do it without thinking. Why? Because we place our faith in the chair that it will not fall. It is the same simple faith when we put our trust or belief/faith in Jesus is the Son of God. It is through Him we are saved.

The Purpose of My Life

You might ask, How can I find God? The Bible says in John 14:6, *"Jesus says unto him, 'I am the Way, the Truth, and the Life: no man comes unto the Father, but by Me.'"*

The Lord Jesus Christ is both man and God. When you trust in the Lord, your life is united with God.

Christ is the only way to Heaven. There is no other way.

January 16

My Purpose as a Christian

When you become a Christian you are a child of God.

"But as many as received him, to them gave he power to become the sons of God, even to them that believe on His name" (John 1:12).

By nature you were a child of wrath, children of this world. As His child you can call Him "Father." All the children of God are born again. As a woman you now are a daughter of God Almighty. Praise His name!

My Purpose as a Christian

As a Christian you have access to God by prayer and by the Holy Scriptures.

"For through Him we both have access by one Spirit unto the Father" (Eph. 2:18). Our access is the Holy Spirit. We draw nigh unto God through the Lord Jesus Christ, by the help of the Holy Spirit, who dwells in you.

My Purpose as a Christian

When you become a Christian the Holy Spirit immediately indwells you.

> *"The Spirit itself bears witness with our spirit, that we are the children of God"* (Rom. 8:16).

> *"But ye are not in the flesh, but in the Spirit, if so be that the Spirit of God dwell in you. Now if any man have not the Spirit of Christ, he is none of His"* (Rom. 8:9).

He dwells in you until the day you enter Heaven. The Lord Jesus Christ sent his Holy Spirit to guide and comfort you.

My Purpose as a Christian

Upon being *"born again,"* you are also sealed by the Holy Spirit.

> *"In whom ye also trusted, after that ye heard the word of truth, the gospel of your salvation: in whom also after that ye believed, ye were sealed with that Holy Spirit of promise"* (Eph. 1:13).

The Holy Spirit is holy Himself, and He makes us holy. That is, we are separated and set apart for God.

My Purpose as a Christian

When we are saved, the Bible says we are sealed by the Holy Spirit unto the day of redemption.

"And grieve not the Holy Spirit of God, whereby ye are sealed unto the day of redemption" (Eph. 4:30).

We do not have to ask for the Holy Spirit because all true believers are sealed to the day of redemption the day you arrive in Heaven with a new body.

My Purpose as a Christian

As a Christian you now have a new citizenship and your home is now heaven.

> *"For our conversation* [citizenship] *is in heaven; from whence also we look for the Saviour, the Lord Jesus Christ: who shall change our vile body, that it may be fashioned like unto His glorious body, according to the working whereby He is able even to subdue all thing unto Himself..."* (Phil. 3:20).

We are pilgrims passing through this world. We are not to get caught up with this world because it is not home to those who love the Lord.

My Purpose as a Christian

When we trust in the Lord as our Saviour, we become a new creation.

> *"Therefore if any man be in Christ, he is a new creature: old things are passed away; behold all thing are become new"* (2 Cor. 5:17).

That means you can get rid of the old garbage that has hindered you in the past. You have a new heart, a new name and a new nature. Old thoughts, old practices and old habits are passed away.

ℳy 𝒫urpose as a Christian

When you place your faith in Christ you become a servant of God.

"But now being made free from sin, and become servants to God, ye have your fruit [benefit] *unto holiness, and the end everlasting life"* (Rom. 6:22).

You were once a servant to sin, bad thoughts, lying, cheating, gossiping, etc. Upon conversion you become the servant of righteousness—you shake off the yoke of sin and turn to be a servant of God.

My Purpose as a Christian

When you are converted to Christ you become a priest.

"But ye are a chosen generation, a royal priesthood, an holy nation, a peculiar people: that ye should show forth the praises of Him who has called you out of darkness into His marvellous light" (1 Pet. 2:9).

A priest is to be separate from sin, to be consecrated to God and to offer up to God worship and praise that is acceptable to God through His Word.

My Purpose as a Christian

Upon receiving Christ as your Saviour, you are baptized into Christ's body.

> *"For by one Spirit are we all baptized into one body, whether we be Jews or Gentiles, whether we be bond or free; and have been all made to drink into one Spirit"* (1 Cor. 12:13).

Christ is the head and we, the believers, are the body or the church. All believers have one thing in common—we have put our faith in Christ.

January 26

My Purpose as a Christian

You become a possessor of eternal life.

"And I give unto them eternal life; and they shall never perish, neither shall any man pluck them out of my hand" (John 10:28).

You are in God's hands; no one can pluck you out. You are safe in the hands of Jesus. Your salvation is not in your keeping, but in the keeping of Jesus Christ and you are preserved in Him.

My Purpose as a Christian

As a woman you may ask, Why do I need to study the Bible?

The Bible is a guide book. It provides *"light"* for our pathway on this earth. *"Thy word is a lamp unto my feet, and a light unto my path"* (Ps. 119:105).

As a guide book it will keep us walking on the right path.

January 28

Your Purpose as a Christian

The Bible teaches us about holiness, which God requires.

"Thy word have I hid in mine heart, that I might not sin against thee" (Ps. 119:11).

If we store God's Word in our hearts and minds, it will keep us from sin.

My Purpose as a Christian

Reading and studying the Bible helps our faith.

"So then faith cometh by hearing, and hearing by the word of God" (Rom. 10:17).

Saturating our minds will also keeps us from evil and from error. We will learn to be wary of false ideas that man projects. The Bible has many prophecies of the Lord's first coming and the future of the Lord's second coming. The Holy Spirit will guide us to walk the Christian walk.

January 30

My Purpose as a Christian

As a young woman you may want to know what path the Lord has for your life. You may want to know how to develop wholesome friendships or how to witness to your friends at school. As a teenager you will be interested in sex and marriage. In the book of Proverbs you will find your answers to life and relationships.

"The fear of the Lord is the beginning of knowledge: but fools despise wisdom and instruction" (Prov. 1:7).

My Purpose as a Christian

As a wife you will want to make your husband happy and to have a contented home. The Song of Solomon is a beautiful love story that you might want to read with your husband. It is a study of love and intimacy. There is a whole section in Proverbs 31 about an excellent wife.

There are many of examples of good and bad mothers. We can learn from both what to do and not to do.

February 1

My Purpose as a Christian

When we trust the Lord Jesus Christ as our Saviour, we become a friend of God.

> *"Henceforth I call you not servants; for the servant knoweth not what his lord doeth: but I have called you friends; for all things I have heard of my Father I have made known unto you"* (John 15:15).

Once we were an enemy of God because God hates sin. Now we are His friend, He wants to communicate and reveal His plan for us.

My Purpose as a Christian

Each woman, saved by grace, has her name is written in heaven.

> *"Notwithstanding in this rejoice not that the spirits are subject unto you; but rather rejoice, because your names are written in heaven"* (Luke 10:20).

It is also called the Lamb's Book of Life or the Book of Life. The great white throne judgment in Revelation 20:11-15 says that those whose names are *"not found in the Book of Life"* are *"cast in the lake of fire* [forever]."

My Purpose as a Christian

As women who have become believers in Christ we will be called a believer or saint.

> *"Unto the church of God which is at Corinth, to them that are sanctified in Christ Jesus, called to be saints, with all that in every place call upon the name of Jesus Christ our Lord..."* (1 Cor. 1:2).

The church is a called-out people. They are a sanctified people—set apart for Christ. They are to be devoted, holy, cleansed, and pure.

My Purpose as a Christian

Each of us will want to own her own Bible. Help is available at a Bible bookstore or from another believer. The Bible is the Word of God and when we read it, we must ask God to reveal it to us, to help us understand the sacred writings.

> *"For this cause also thank we God with ceasing, because, when ye received the Word of God which ye heard of us, you received it not as the word of men, but as it is in truth, the Word of God, which effectually worketh also in you that believe"* (1 Thess. 2:13).

February 5

My Purpose as a Christian

As women studying the Bible, we should have a willing mind. John 7:17 says *"If any man will do his will, he shall know of the doctrine, whether it be of God, or whether I speak of myself."*

After studying the word we need to be willing to obey it knowing that this is a word from the Lord Himself.

My Purpose as a Christian

When studying the Word of God we need to have an obedient mind.

> *"But be ye doers of the Word, and not hearers only, deceiving your own selves. For if any be a hearer of the Word, and not a doer, He is like unto a man beholding his natural face in a glass. For he beholds himself, and goes his own way, and straightway forgets what manner of man he was"* (Jas. 1: 22,23).

February 7

My Purpose as a Christian

As women we want to be teachable like Mary of Bethany who sat at the Lord's feet. Matthew 11:25 says:

> *"At that time Jesus answered and said, 'I thank Thee, O Father, Lord of heaven and earth, because Thou hast hid these things from the wise and prudent, and hast revealed them unto babes."*

When I got saved at the age of twelve, an older man instructed me to read the gospels first, and the Psalms. We must ask God to reveal the passage we just read.

My Purpose as a Christian

There are many ways of studying the Bible. At first it might be wise to start off in Genesis and work through to then see the whole plan of God. In the Old Testament we learn about God and in the New Testament we learn about the Lord Jesus Christ.

When studying the biographies of the Bible we see that the men and the women of the Bible are very much like we are.

My Purpose as a Christian

We can also study topics of the Bible such as God, man, Jesus Christ, sin, the fall of man, heaven, and hell. Try studying and learning what a New Testament church is.

We can study other women to learn about their faith in God. Some might say, "I am only a woman." That is a humble stand and since to be humble is to be like Jesus, who said *"I am meek and lowly in heart...."* (Matt. 11:29), we can learn about the faithful women in the Bible.

My Purpose as a Christian

There are many helps for studying the Bible. Some examples are:

1. *Vines Complete Expository*
2. Dictionary of Old & New Testament Words
3. *Unger's Bible Dictionary*
4. *Strong's Exhaustive Concordance*
5. *Believer's Bible Commentary*
6. PC Study Bible 3.0 (computer)

And there are others.

_____

_____

_____

_____

_____

_____

_____

My Purpose as a Christian

We should read our Bibles every day.

In 1 Peter 2:2 we read, *"As newborn babes, desire the sincere milk of the word, that you may grow thereby."*

The mind is strengthened and nourished by Bible reading. This enables us to fight the good fight of faith.

We should aim to read a portion from the Bible every day. Don't leave Bible reading to Sundays only. We don't want to stay a baby all our life but we want to grow in the Lord.

When we go to Heaven we will meet Hosea and won't we be embarrassed if we did not read his book?

My Purpose as a Christian

We need to read each text carefully, we must not take a verse out and build a doctrine around it.

> *"Till I* [the Lord] *come, give attendance to reading, to exhortation, to doctrine"* (1 Tim. 4:13).

Some Christians want to do all the talking to God, but they don't want to listen to what God has to say. They are Christians who don't want to bother with doctrine. We need to learn about the Deity of Christ, The Virgin Birth, His atoning death, the new birth, eternal life, and the coming of the Lord

We are called upon to believe these great truths of Scripture.

My Purpose as a Christian

We are to meditate on the text.

> *"This book of the law shall not depart out of thy mouth; but thou shalt meditate therein day and night, that thou mayest observe to do according to all that is written there in..."* (Josh. 1:8).

The Bible is God's infallible pattern. Obey it all, or admit that you are denying the Lordship of Christ.

My Purpose as a Christian

Many missionaries when they are opening up a new area will begin teaching from the book of Genesis, go through the Old Testament which teaches us all about God and His ways, and then move into the New Testament to introduce Christ to their hearers. The Old Testament is not our source of doctrine; nevertheless, divine principles never change.

> *"For whatsoever things were written aforetime were written for our learning, that we through patience and comfort of the scriptures might have hope"* (Rom. 15:4).

February 15

My Purpose as a Christian

Some people are horrified at marking or underlining key verses in the Bible. I find it helpful when I have a Bible study with other women, these verses jump out and help illustrate certain points of interest where we are studying. In this way my Bible becomes a study book. My memory does not serve me any more so this is a great help. And I also found that getting a big print Bible is another help.

Verses jump out at me that I don't remember reading before. The Bible is always refreshing to read again and again.

My Purpose as a Christian

Try to memorize key gospel verses and meditate on them, so we can give an answer to anyone who is inquiring about the Scriptures and the Lord.

Mary the mother of our Lord sang a beautiful song to God in Luke 1:46-55. It starts off with *"My soul doth magnify the Lord, and my spirit has rejoiced in God my Saviour."* Mary's God was her Saviour and as a young girl she knew the Scriptures in the Old Testament. She magnified the Lord and sang about the great things that God had done for His people.

So she knew the scriptures well!

My Purpose as a Christian

In 2 Timothy 3:16 it states:

"All scripture is given by inspiration of God, and is profitable for doctrine, for reproof, for correction, for instruction in righteousness that the man of God may be perfect, thoroughly furnished unto all good works."

"Doctrine": God's thoughts of what is right according to His will.

"Reproof": God showing man he is not right.

"Correction": God putting man right.

"Instruction": God teaching man to do what is right.

My Purpose as a Christian

The first four books of the New Testament, give the gospel of our Lord Jesus Christ—His birth, His walk, His death and His resurrection.

The book of Acts chronicles the beginning of the Church, followed by the Epistles which are for our benefit today and then the book of Revelation—a coming day.

February 19

My Purpose as a Christian

As a woman of God your prayer life is most important. God speaks through His Word and we can talk to God.

"And all things, whatsoever you shall ask in prayer, believing, you shall receive" (Matt. 21:22).

The first prayer God wants to hear from you, is "God be merciful to me a sinner." But when we become Christians we have access to the Father, in Jesus' name. We ask for what we need or for the desires of our heart according to God's will.

My Purpose as a Christian

Our prayers should be made up of: Praise.

"After this manner therefore pray ye: Our Father which art in heaven, Hallowed be Thy name" (Matt. 6:9).

God is holy and majestic, but He is also loving and personal. We are not to use God's name lightly, but to remember He is a holy God and reverence should be maintained.

"Holy and reverend is His name" (Ps. 111:9).

"Holy and reverend" belongs only to God. A man should never be named Reverend because this belongs to God only.

My Purpose as a Christian

And our prayers should be seasoned with... thanksgiving.

"Offer unto God thanksgiving; and pay thy vows unto the most High" (Ps. 50:14).

"Continue in prayer, and watch in the same with thanksgiving" (Col. 4:2).

Thanksgiving is our occupation with our blessings. Prayer is our occupation with our needs and with others.

"Give us this day our daily bread" (Matt. 6:11).

Worship is our occupation with the Lord Himself. Both the worship of the Lord and the work of the Lord must be guided by the word of the Lord.

My Purpose as a Christian

Our prayers should include confession of sin. Matthew 6:12 & 13 says:

> *"And forgive us our debts as we forgive our debtors and lead us not into temptation, but deliver us from evil..."*

As long as we are in these bodies we shall be tempted to sin, but God has promised that He won't allow us to be tempted beyond our endurance.

Keep short accounts with God, we must confess our sin right away, and forgive others who trespass against us. If we don't forgive others, why should God forgive us?

My Purpose as a Christian

We pray because the Lord taught us to pray.

"After this manner therefore pray ye..." (Matt. 6:9).

We are never to give up.

"Ask, and it shall be given you; seek, and ye shall find; knock, and it shall be opened unto you" (Matt. 7:7).

Remember the Saviour never quits praying for us, and we should never quit praying. The Lord Himself said to His disciples: *"If you abide in Me, and My words abide in you, you shall ask what you will, and it shall be done unto you"* (John 15:7).

The key is to abide in Christ and to ask according to His will.

My Purpose as a Christian

In Luke 18:1 we are told to always pray and not to faint.

We need to constantly put our needs before God as we live for Him each day. We always believe He will answer our prayers. God may have a good reason for the delay; we must not think of God being neglectful. If we live by faith, we are not to give up.

I heard of a lady who prayed 75 years for her brother's salvation. At the 11th hour he was converted. Keep praying for those loved ones!!

My Purpose as a Christian

We need to pray in time of need.

"Pray without ceasing" (1 Thess. 5:17).

We cannot spend all our time on our knees, but we can have a prayerful attitude all the time. It means short prayers to God.

"Let us therefore come boldly unto the throne of grace, that we may obtain mercy, and find grace to help in time of need" (Heb. 4:16).

God is your counselor and friend; do not be afraid to approach God.

My Purpose as a Christian

God is our Father and when we enter His presence we must have faith that God is a rewarder of those who sincerely seek Him.

> *"But without faith it is impossible to please Him; for He that comes to God must believe that He is, and that He is a rewarder of them that diligently seek Him"* (Heb. 11:6).

How many mistakes and wrong choices in life are made because we do not wait on God in prayer? We must bathe every decision in prayer, asking God for guidance.

February 27

My Purpose as a Christian

We are to pray in the name of the Lord Jesus Christ. This is how our prayers should end.

> *"Jesus said unto him, 'I am the Way, the Truth, and the Life; no man comes unto the Father, but by Me'"* (John 14:6).

Christ finished His work at Calvary, so we have no claims on God, only through Christ. Christ is our High Priest who intercedes for us. In Jesus' name, amen!

My Purpose as a Christian

We are to pray in the Spirit.

> *"Praying always with all prayer and supplication in the Spirit, and watching thereunto with all perseverance and supplication for all saints"* (Eph. 6:18).

Every time we hear about a need, we should make it a habit to pray right away for that need. In this way we can make prayer our life. We should ask for direction in the morning before we start our day. This will direct our paths. Remember prayer defeats our enemies.

My Purpose as a Christian

We are to pray for all men, especially those in authority.

"I exhort therefore, that, first of all supplication, prayers, intercession, and giving of thanks, be made for all men; for kings, and for all that are in authority; that we may lead a quiet and peaceable life in all godliness and honesty" (1 Tim. 2:1,2).

Even in terrible persecution we are to pray for our leaders. We are to pray for their salvation. And it is our duty and responsibility to pray for the household of faith.

My Purpose as a Christian

We are to pray for the sick.

> *"Is any sick among you? Let him call for the elders of the church; and let them pray over him, anointing him with oil in the name of the Lord: and the prayer of faith shall save the sick, and the Lord shall raise him up; and if he have committed sins, they shall be forgiven him. Confess your faults one to another, and pray one for another, that you may be healed. The effectual fervent prayer of a righteous man availeth much"* (Jas. 5:14-16).

Members of the body of Christ should be counted on for support in the time of sickness and suffering.

Corporate prayer is essential in the life of the church.

My Purpose as a Christian

We can pray for wisdom (1 Kgs. 3:5-12).

Pray for a longer life (Isa. 38:1-5).

Pray for a prosperous journey (Rom. 1:10).

We can pray for every believer to be made perfect in Christ Jesus (Col. 1:28).

Pray for them that despise us and for our enemies (Matt. 5:44).

My Purpose as a Christian

We have to be careful we do not hinder our prayers.

> *"But let him ask in faith, nothing wavering for he that wavereth is like a wave of the sea driven with the wind and tossed. For let not that man think that he shall receive anything of the Lord"* (Jas. 1:6,7).

If we doubt, then we are not convinced that God's way is best. We treat prayer like human advice. The cure for this is full commitment to God's way.

My Purpose as a Christian

When we pray we are to have a forgiving spirit.

"And when you stand praying, forgive, if you aught against any: that your Father also which is in heaven may forgive you your trespasses" (Mark 11:15).

We must make sure our prayer is in the will of God.

My Purpose as a Christian

For our personal prayers, the Bible says we are to be alone with Him.

> *"But thou, when thou prayest, enter into thy closet and when thou has shut thy door, pray to thy Father which is in secret"* (Matt. 6:6).

Our minds can wander quite quickly, so the Lord knows we need a very private place without disturbances.

March 6

My Purpose as a Christian

For a woman to be a godly life she must have a Spirit-filled life. As a believer we are to abdicate our life to the Holy Spirit.

"And be not drunk with wine, wherein is excess; but be filled with the Spirit" (Eph. 5:18).

Wine has harmful effects but the filling of the Holy Spirit has a positive effect.

My Purpose as a Christian

Being filled with the Spirit expresses our:

> *"Giving thanks always for all things unto God and the Father in the name of our Lord Jesus Christ"* (Eph. 5:20).

Being filled with the Spirit empowers us to live difficult circumstances with a thankful heart and gives us power to live a victorious life. The filling of the Spirit is an individual blessing.

My Purpose as a Christian

Being filled with the Spirit requires submission. A lot of Christians have a hard time with this, but we must remember the Lord had to submit to the Father.

"Submitting yourselves one to another in the fear of God" (Eph. 5:21).

We honour Christ by following his example and being willing to submit to others.

My Purpose as a Wife

In a marriage, both wife and husband are to submit to each other.

> "Wives, submit yourselves unto your own husbands, as unto the Lord" (Eph. 5:22).

The wife is to reverence her husband. She is not to be a doormat, but can speak her mind, letting the final decision be his if there is a deadlock.

The wife should be willing to follow her husband's leadership in Christ.

March 10

The Purpose of my Husband

As husbands are head of the home, they are told to love their wives.

"Husbands, love your wives, even as Christ also loved the church, and gave himself for it" (Eph. 5:25).

"So ought men to love their wives as their own bodies. He that loves his wife loves himself" (Eph. 5:28).

These verses are telling us to care for each other, to learn to know each other's needs. We are to be one.

The Purpose of my Children

If our children are believers they will want to honour and obey both mother and father.

> *"Children obey your parents in the Lord: for this is right. Honour your father and mother; which is the first commandment with promise"* (Eph. 6:1,2).

There is a difference between obeying and honouring your parents. To obey means we must to do as we are told. To honour our parents shows love and respect, and this should continue all the days of our life.

My Purpose as a Parent

For a mother, her children are her mission field.

She must bring them up in the Lord and be one with her husband in discipline and training of the children. Ephesians 6:4 addresses the father, but the mother can pay attention to this too.

> *"And, ye fathers, provoke not your children to wrath: but bring them up in the nurture and admonition of the Lord."*

"Nurture": training, serving, and education

"Admonition": to administer mild reproof

My Purpose as an Employee

Since we represent Christ to our employer, we must give our best and our integrity should shine.

> *"Servants, be obedient to them that are your masters according to the flesh, with fear and trembling, in singleness of your heart, as unto Christ; not with eye service, as men-pleasers; but as the servants of Christ, doing the will of God from the heart"* (Eph. 6:5-7).

We must make sure we do not rob our employer of his time or even of a small elastic band!

My Purpose as an Employer

We are to treat our employees with respect, and not to play favourites.

> *"And you masters, do the same things unto them, forbearing threatening: knowing that your Master also is in heaven; neither is there respect of persons with him"* (Eph. 6:8,9).

Please don't treat your employee like a machine. Pay him or her a fair wage.

My Purpose as a Christian

The filling of the Spirit requires daily exercise.

If we have violated and departed from the will of God, we must be restored. We are to walk as children of light; our talk should be without foul language or gossip. Neither should we be talking foolishly.

> *"For ye were sometimes darkness, but now are ye light in the Lord: walk as children of light"* (Eph. 5:8).

My Purpose as a Woman

What is the will of God for me as a woman?

The first thing that God wants for a man and woman is to be saved.

> *"Who will have all men to be saved, and to come unto the knowledge of the truth"* (1 Tim. 2:4).

This is the most important decision in our life—nothing else matters. Remember this decision is for eternity and also God intends it to be a blessing in our life as long as we live on this earth.

My Purpose as a Christian

There are different aspects of God's will. God's moral will, for example, is seen in the Ten Commandments: thou shalt not do this or thou shalt do this.

"Thou shalt not kill. Honour thy father and thy mother" (Ex. 20 1-17).

We should obey these commandments today, even though we are not under the law, but under grace.

My Purpose as a Christian

It is God's will that we obey the powers that be. If we drive beyond the speed limit we are taking ourselves out of God's hand because He put in power the people make laws for our safety and benefit.

> *"Let every soul be subject unto the higher powers. For there is no power but of God: the powers that be are ordained of God"* (Rom. 13:1).

People that are in authority are ministers of God (Rom. 13:1-7).

My Purpose as a Christian

There are quite a few instances in the New Testament where God says: *"This is My will."* Every time we come across this phrase, we should write it down in a notebook and thus will learn the will of God for our life.

God's moral will will not lead us to anything that is in conflict with His moral law. For example, He will never lead a husband to leave his wife for a more spiritual wife. When we live in obedience to God's will we are then in step with God's thoughts and God's ways. We will have a hard time discovering God's personal will if we ignore His moral will.

My Purpose as a Christian

In God's will there is the law of sowing and reaping. God has given us His principles as a check and balance in the decision-making.

> *"Be not deceived; God is not mocked: for whatsoever a man soweth, that shall he also reap"* (Gal. 6:7).

Even when Christ forgives our sins, we will have to reap what we sowed. We still have to pay the consequences of sin.

My Purpose as a Christian

When wanting to make a decision, I might ask myself: Is this a wise thing to do in the light of...

1. My present state of mind?
2. My relationship with my mother or husband?
3. What kind of marriage I want or career?
4. How will it affect my ability to serve God?

Read the book of Proverbs. It is full of wisdom about everyday life. God is interested in all aspects of our life and He wants us to rely on Him for wisdom. Pray for wisdom!

March 22

My Purpose as a Christian

To know the mind of God is to know the Scriptures and to remember we are not our own, we were bought with a price. We forsook our own way when we received Jesus Christ as Saviour.

"For you are bought with a price: therefore glorify God in your body, and in your spirit, which are God's" (1 Cor. 6:20).

Since we belong to God we must not go against His standard of living.

My Purpose as a Christian

If we are in doubt about the will of God in our life, it is to our benefit to get godly counsel from an experienced believer.

"Without counsel purposes are disappointed: but in the multitude of counselors they are established" (Prov. 15:22).

Make sure that the counselor's life and counsel lines up with God's way.

My Purpose as a Christian

One of the purposes of the Holy Spirit is to show you the truth, but if we have deliberate sin in our life, finding God's will will be frustrating.

"If I regard iniquity in my heart, the Lord will not hear me" (Ps. 66:18).

We need light for only one step at a time. As we obey the light that God has already given us then He will show us further light.

My Purpose as a Christian

The will of God in our life is that we be filled with the Spirit (Eph. 5:18). We must now be determined to *"Walk worthy of the Lord."*

Is *"thus saith the Lord"* our monitor? If so we are becoming rooted and grounded in the faith.

> *"Wherefore be ye not unwise, but understanding what the will of the Lord is"* (Eph. 5:17).

If we know what God wants us to do, we must act upon it.

My Purpose as a Christian

When we made Jesus Christ Lord of our lives, we wanted salvation, forgiveness, heaven, love and the Lord Jesus. With this we may have the pleasure of suffering for His sake.

> *"For unto you it is given in the behalf of Christ, not only to believe on Him, but also to suffer for His sake"* (Phil. 1:29).

When we represent Christ, we may have to suffer reproach, and suffering verifies that we belong to Him.

My Purpose as a Christian

How does suffering come?

1. Through our own mistakes and sin.

2. Mistakes and sins of others.

Temptations:

> "There has no temptation taken you but such as is common to man: but God is faithful, who will not suffer you to be tempted above that you are able; but will with the temptation also make a way to escape, that you may be able to bear it" (1 Cor. 10:13).

We sometimes suffer through God's providential dealings.

March 28

My Purpose as a Christian

There are many reasons we could be called upon to suffer for Christ. Read Hebrews 12:3-13 (The Father's chastening).

Suffering is for our profit, to promote holiness and it produces godly traits. One of the purposes of suffering is that it proves we are God's children.

> *"Yea, and all that will live godly in Christ Jesus shall suffer persecution"* (2 Tim. 3:12).

My Purpose as a Christian

Suffering encourages us to draw near to Christ. Of course we could rebel instead of submit.

When the apostle Paul was afflicted with a disease, he asked the Lord three times to take this affliction away from him. But the Lord's answer was: *"My grace is sufficient for thee; for my strength is made perfect in weakness"* (2 Cor. 12:9).

In our weakness we confirm God's strength for us to endure the affliction.

March 30

My Purpose as a Christian

It is the will of God that we be a witness for Him. In Matthew 28:19-20 every believer is commissioned to be a witness.

> *"Go ye therefore, and teach all nations, baptizing them in the name of the Father; and of the Son, and of the Holy Ghost. Teaching them to observe all thing whatsoever I have commanded you: and, lo I am with you always, even unto the end of the world. Amen."*

We are to go out, not expect people to come in.

_____

_____

_____

_____

_____

_____

My Purpose as a Christian

It is the will of God that we surrender our will to His because Christ surrendered His will to the Father. John 6:38,39 says:

> *"For I came down from heaven, not to do mine own will, but the will of him that sent me. And this is the Father's will which has sent me, that of all which he has given me I should lose nothing, but should raise it up again at the last day."*

Jesus worked with God the Father. When we follow Jesus we will want to follow the will of God and not our earthly desires.

April 1

My Purpose as a Christian

It is God's will for us to be servants.

In Mark 10:44, 45 we are called to be servants.

"And whosoever of you will be the chiefest, shall be servant of all. For even the Son of man came not be ministered unto, but to minister, [serve] and to give his life a ransom for many."

To be a servant of Christ is a high calling. Christ was the perfect servant.

My Purpose as a Christian

Sanctification is the will of God for every believer. Sanctification basically means separation.

Believers are eternally set apart for God by redemption. We become a saint and holy the moment we believed in the Lord (1 Thess. 4:1-4).

We are to separate ourselves from evil, and separate ourselves unto God.

April 3

My Purpose as a Christian

How are we to be sanctified? By the Word of God.

"Sanctify them [the believers] *through thy truth: thy word is truth"* (John 17:17).

The word of God cleanses, purifies and reveals sin in our lives. It is our job to seek out the sin, judge it, pray for cleansing and to live a holy life.

The Word reveals sin and the blood cleanses it away—result: sanctification.

My Purpose as a Christian

To live a sanctified life we are not to be unequally yoked together with unbelievers.

> *"Be ye not unequally yoked together with unbelievers: for what fellowship has righteousness with unrighteousness? And what communion has light with darkness?"* (2 Cor. 6:14).

We have relatives that might be unsaved, and we want to them to become believers but we do not need to walk their walk nor talk their talk. We need to show them we have a new life in Christ.

My Purpose as a Christian

It is God's purpose that we are to marry in the Lord. We are not to marry an unbeliever.

You would not be able to:
1. Read your Bible and pray together
2. Talk of spiritual things

How can light have friendship with darkness? How are we going to bring up our children? In light or darkness?

Don't count on this person to become saved!

My Purpose as a Christian

We are not to be yoked in a business partnership. How can the saved person and the unsaved person agree in business methods and ethics?

"Two can only walk together if they are agreed" (Amos 3:3).

The unbeliever cannot rise to the spiritual level of the believer, so the believer will descend and surrender to the unbeliever's level.

My Purpose as a Christian

We are not to be yoked socially. This is the world of clubs and organizations to promote happiness and mutual well-being. A lot of organizations are praiseworthy. Whose standard of conduct will prevail? Whose standard of conversation or ideals must be adopted? 1 Corinthians 6:15 says:

> *"And what concord hath Christ with Belial? Or what part has he that believeth with an infidel?"*

_____

_____

_____

_____

_____

_____

My Purpose as a Christian

The ecclesiastical yoke: Church fellowship should be restricted to those who have been saved by God's grace. There are religious systems around us that are devised by men's wisdom, where saved and unsaved meet together for the "public worship" of God. How can these two worship together, or testify together, or pray and serve together?

> *"Wherefore come out from among them, and be ye separate, saith the Lord, and touch not the unclean [unsaved] thing; and I will receive you"* (2 Cor. 6:17).

April 9

My Purpose as a Christian

"And have no fellowship with the unfruitful works of darkness, but rather reprove them" (Eph. 5:11).

We must not practice them ourselves and we must not countenance others in the practice of them. Often our silence is taken for approval. We need to make a stand for what is right.

We are not to adopt a lifestyle that recommends bad behaviour.

My Purpose as a Christian

We are to keep away from anything that denies the person and work of Christ.

There are people who reason that the Lord Jesus Christ could not have been both God and man. 2 John 7 says:

> *"For many deceivers are entered into the world, who confess not that Jesus Christ is come in the flesh. This is a deceiver and an antichrist."*

My Purpose as a Christian

Service, suffering and separating us to God, is not for years to come, but for ages to come. Our heavenly Father has the eternal ages in view. Why? Because in Revelation 5:10 we shall reign on earth with Christ. Our lifetime is training time for reigning time. God is fitting us for responsibilities and authority in His Kingdom.

"And hast made us unto our God kings and priests: and we shall reign on the earth."

My Purpose as a Christian

As godly women walking in the Spirit and yielding to Him we will experience the *"Fruit of the Spirit."*

> *"But the fruit of the Spirit is love, joy, peace, longsuffering, gentleness, goodness, faith, meekness, temperance: against such there is no law"* (Gal. 5:22-23).

We must recognize that these traits are all found in Christ. We must imitate Him and the result is our love for God and man.

My Purpose as a Christian

LOVE: *"And we have known and believed the love that God has to us. God is love; and He that dwells in love dwells in God, and God in Him"* (1 John 4:16).

This is divine love and it is God-ward. If we love, we will serve each other. We are to love God and our neighbours as ourself.

> *"By this shall all men know that you are my disciples, if you have love one to another"* (John 13:35).

1 Corinthians 13:1-13 says love is essential. It is more than prophecy, knowledge, mysteries and faith.

My Purpose as a Christian

JOY: Philippians is an epistle of joy.

"Rejoice in the Lord always" (Phil. 4:4).

This is how we have triumph over impossible odds. It is a deep sense of gladness and we are to be cheerful in our conversation to each other.

It is the privilege of believers to rejoice not just in the good times but also in all things, at all times—good or bad. Our Saviour is our source of joy.

My Purpose as a Christian

PEACE: This is the peace of God.

> *"And let the peace of God rule in your hearts, to the which also you are called in one body; and be ye thankful"* (Col. 3:15).

This peace stems from the knowledge and acceptance of the will of God in our life.

> *"My times are in thy hand: deliver me from the hand of mine enemies, and from them that persecute me"* (Ps. 31:15).

My Purpose as a Christian

LONGSUFFERING: As a believer we are to be patient with people and to have self-restraint in the face of provocation.

"With all lowliness and meekness, with longsuffering, forbearing one another in love" (Eph. 4:2).

The world watches us. Can they see Christ in us? Remember we are Christ's ambassadors on earth.

My Purpose as a Christian

GENTLENESS: The Lord was gracious and kind, so we should be also. We are to display a gracious attitude, even when we are tempted to be abrasive.

"To speak evil of no man, to be no brawlers, but gentle, showing all meekness unto all men" (Tit. 3:2).

If we find faults in other believers, we should be gentle and kind with them. We should pray for them and make friends with them.

My Purpose as a Christian

GOODNESS: We should be full of good works and ready to do good as we have opportunity to do so.

"And I myself also am persuaded of you, my brethren, that ye also are full of goodness, filled with all knowledge, able also to admonish one another" (Rom. 15:4).

Let us remember the goodness of God!

My Purpose as a Christian

FAITH: People should have confidence in me and know that I can be relied on for honesty and justice.

Read Hebrews 11, for it is a great chapter of the faith of men and woman in God.

> *"But without faith it is impossible to please Him; for he that cometh to God must believe that He is, and that He is a rewarder of them that diligently seek him"* (Heb. 11:6).

Faith is fundamental to the believer's conduct for we are saved by faith (Eph. 2:8).

My Purpose as a Christian

MEEKNESS: We must not associate meekness with weakness. Weakness is a lack of courage and strength. Meekness is due to a person's conscious choice. It is strength and courage under control, coupled with kindness.

> *"I therefore, the prisoner of the Lord, beseech you that you walk worthy of the vocation wherewith you are called, with all lowliness and meekness, with longsuffering, forbearing one another in love.*
>
> *"Endeavouring to keep the unity of the Spirit in the bond of peace"* (Eph. 4:13).

My Purpose as a Christian

TEMPERANCE: We should be expressing self-control and moderation in food, drink, dress, fashion or any other enjoyment of life.

Also indicated is the self-control that masters all kinds of sensual desires such as sexual desire and the desire for material things.

> *"Let us lay aside every weight, and the sin which does so easily beset us, and let us run with patience the race that is set before us. Looking unto Jesus the Author and Finisher of our faith..."* (Heb. 12:1).

My Purpose as a Christian

As a believer we will want to have fellowship with other believers. In Acts 2:41,42, we have an outline of how we have fellowship with God as a collective body of Christians in a local church.

> *"Then they that gladly received his word were baptized: and the same day there were added unto them about three thousand souls. And they continued steadfastly in the apostles' doctrine and fellowship, and in breaking of bread, and in prayers."*

God puts us into a family.

April 23

My Purpose as a Christian

The local church where we attend should have the following qualifications:

1. Restricted to Christian membership (Acts 2:47).
2. Gathered unto the name of the Lord Jesus Christ (Matt. 18:20). No other name!!
3. Graced by the Lord in the midst. *"There am I in midst"* (Matt. 18:2).

My Purpose as a Christian

The local church qualifications:

4. Subject to the Lordship of Christ

> *"Therefore let all the house of Israel know assuredly, that God has made that same Jesus, whom you have crucified, both Lord and Christ"* (Acts 2:36).

We are to give Him the place of Lord in our hearts (1 Pet. 3:15).

The Holy Spirit teaches us to recognize Christ as Lord in the assembly (1 Cor. 12:3).

My Purpose as a Christian

The local church is to be guided by Elders (1 Pet. 5:1-3).

The church is to be instructed by ministers, deacons, evangelists, pastors and teachers. Notice that they are all in the plural. There is no room for a one-man ministry!

Ephesians 4:11,12 lists the gifts to the church for the gospel, edification, pastoral ministry and exhortation.

My Purpose as a Christian

There is the priesthood of believers.

This is regarding worship when we come to remember the Lord at His table. We are to offer up praise and worship.

> *"By him therefore let us offer the sacrifice of praise to God continually, that is, the fruit of our lips giving thanks to his name"* (Heb. 13:15).

1 Peter 2:5,9 says that we are a holy priesthood and a royal priesthood. We are to present our bodies a living sacrifice (Rom. 12:1).

My Purpose as a Christian

In Acts 2:41 *"they gladly received his word."*

The first thing we must do to have fellowship with God is to trust the Lord Jesus Christ as our Saviour and Lord.

There are Christians who have *"crossed over the Red Sea"* (for salvation) but have no desire to cross over Jordan and enter into the land (the fellowship of the Lord's people and the responsibilities of the Local church).

My Purpose as a Christian

Our Lord gave a command to His disciples before He left, saying:

> *"Go ye into all the world, and preach the gospel to every creature. He that believeth and is baptized shall be saved; but he that believeth not shall be damned"* (Mark 16:15,16).

After we trust the Lord and want to follow Him, He has requested that we be baptized. All those who have truly repented of their sins and believed in Christ are to be baptized.

Baptism is full immersion under the water. There is no mention in Scripture of sprinkling.

April 29

My Purpose as a Christian

The teaching of baptism is in Romans 6:3-6.

"Know ye not, that so many of us as were baptized into Jesus Christ were baptized into this death? Therefore we are buried with him by baptism into death: that like as Christ was raised up from the dead by the glory of the Father, even so we also should walk in newness of life."

We are telling the world that you want to be identified with Christ—in His death, His burial and His resurrection.

To have fellowship with God we follow Acts 2:41,

"Then they that gladly received his word were baptized."

My Purpose as a Christian

Following the baptism of the new believers in Acts 2:41, we read, *"and the same day there were added unto them about three thousand souls."*

While they were added to the Lord, they were also added to the newly formed church at Jerusalem.

One of the great preservatives in the Christian life is fellowship with other Christians. Remember the church is born again believers!

The place where we meet is just that-a place! The New Testament is the sole authority as to how Christians should gather.

My Purpose as a Christian

When we take God for our God, we must take His people to be our people. Being received into this fellowship of God and His people (the local church) means we are ready to embrace the privileges of our local church life and are ready to accept the responsibilities that go along with the privilege.

"Not forsaking the assembling of ourselves together, as the manner of some is; but exhorting one another: and so much the more, as ye see the day approaching" (Heb. 10:25).

My Purpose as a Christian

"And they continued steadfastly in the apostles' doctrine"
(Acts 2:42).

We learn the apostles' doctrine which governs church life by reading the Epistles. Doctrine means teaching.

That is, whatever the apostles taught the believers they *"persevered in,"* and steadfastly obeyed. The early Christians obeyed what the apostles taught them knowing that apostles were preaching to them the will of God.

My Purpose as a Christian

"And they continued steadfastly in the apostles' doctrine and fellowship" (Acts 2:42).

Fellowship means sharing in common or partnership. Acts 2:44 says, *"And all that believed were together, and had all things common."*

We should study 1 and 2 Corinthians because these two books illustrate the togetherness and fellowship in God's assembly.

My Purpose as a Christian

This fellowship is the common privilege of all true believers. 1 John 1:3 states:

> *"That which we have seen and heard declare we unto you, that you also may have fellowship with us: and truly our fellowship is with the Father, and with his Son Jesus Christ."*

The result of this relationship is the fellowship of being in the family of God.

My Purpose as a Christian

To have fellowship in an assembly of God's people we must have a common understanding of the word of God and a desire to submit to the headship of the Lord Jesus Christ. Colossians 1:18 says:

> *"And he is the head of the body, the church; who is the beginning, the firstborn from the dead; that in all things he might have the preeminence."*

This applies to the local church as well as to the universal church. Only Christ heads the church, no one man, no one elder or pastor.

_____

_____

_____

_____

_____

_____

My Purpose as a Christian

Fellowship, in the New Testament has two sides to it. There is fellowship with God and there is fellowship with other Christians. If we are not enjoying the one aspect of the fellowship, we will not be enjoying the other. They are linked together.

If I do not maintain my fellowship with my heavenly Father through prayer and study of the Bible, it won't be long before I am finding fault with the Christians.

May 7

My Purpose as a Christian

There is the fellowship of giving.

> *"For it hath pleased them of Macedonia and Achaia to make a certain contribution for the poor saints which are at Jerusalem"* (Rom. 15:26).

We can give to needy Christians and also to those who are in the service of the Lord and have no means of livelihood.

A good example of those who are serving the Lord is missionaries.

My Purpose as a Christian

There is the fellowship of prayer.

"Always in every prayer of mine for you all making request with joy, for your fellowship in the gospel from the first day until now" (Phil 1:4,5).

We need to pray for the Christians that we know and hear of all around the world. They need our intercession.

My Purpose as a Christian

Acts 2:42 mentions *"and in breaking of bread, and in prayers."* This is part of our fellowship with God and other believers.

This verse is referring to the Lord's Supper, which is a divine appointment. It should never be second place or held just occasionally.

> *"And upon the first day of the week, when the disciples came together to break bread, Paul preached unto them..."* (Acts 20:7).

My Purpose as a Christian

The Lord Jesus Himself first instituted the breaking of bread in the upper room on the night of His betrayal.

> *"For I have received of the Lord that which also I delivered unto you, That the Lord Jesus the same night in which He was betrayed took bread and when He had given thanks He brake it, and said, Take, eat: this is My body, which is broken for your; this do in remembrance of Me"* (1 Cor. 11:23).

He also took the cup.

My Purpose as a Christian

It is important to *"break bread"* because the Lord commanded it. (1 Cor. 11:24,25)

Three gospels emphasize that the Lord taught it. (Matt. 26:26-28; Mark 14:22-24; Luke 22:19,20).

The Lord had personally revealed to Paul in 1 Corinthians 11:23, that this was to take place in the local church and it was to be observed collectively.

My Purpose as a Christian

The Lord's Supper (Breaking of Bread) according to 1 Corinthians 11:23 is a remembrance of the Lord's death, burial and resurrection.

This meeting is not to minister to other believers but to minister to the heart of God about His Son through reading the Scriptures, hymns pertaining to Christ and worship (prayer) expressing our love for Christ.

My Purpose as a Christian

"...and in prayers" (Acts 2:42).

The theme is the corporate prayer life of the assembly. In Acts 1:14 the local church met together for prayer. This is the power house of God's local church.

Prayer is used by God to promote spiritual growth, bring power into the work as an assembly, lead to the salvation of others in Christ, and with it blessing to Christ's church.

My Purpose as a Woman in the Church

In the universal church, which is Christ's body,

> *"There is neither Jew nor Greek, there is neither bond nor free, there is neither male nor female: for you are all one in Christ Jesus"* (Gal. 3:28).

We are all equal in Christ in the universal church. In the local church there are different roles for men and women *but* we are still equal in God's sight!

My Purpose as a Woman in the Church

The woman of the New Testament church is a priest who is to offer up her praise, prayers, and worship to God in silence.

"Let your women keep silence in the churches, for it is not permitted unto them to speak; but they are commanded to be under obedience, as also saith the law" (1 Cor. 14:34).

Only God hears what you are offering up to Him concerning His Son.

My Purpose as a Woman in the Church

Why are woman to be silent in the church?

1. Christ is the head of the church
2. He is the Bridegroom
3. He is male
4. Only Christ speaks (Rev. 1).
5. The Church is Christ body
6. The Church is the Bride of Christ
7. The Church is female
8. The Church does not speak, only Christ

My Purpose as a Woman in the Church

"Let the woman learn in silence with all subjection. But I suffer not a woman to teach, nor to usurp authority over the man, but to be in silence" (1 Tim. 2:11-12).

If there is a church meeting and men are present, then the women are to be silent. In Acts 18:24-26 Paul's commends coworker Priscilla, who taught Apollo, a preacher, in her home.

My Purpose as a Woman in the Church

In 1 Corinthians 11:3 we have the government of God in the assembly. We have Christ who represents God, man who represents Christ, and the woman who represents man.

When the man gets up to pray, worship, teach or preach, he represents Christ whose glory is to shine forth—the man's head is to be uncovered,

> *"Every man praying or prophesying having his head covered dishonoureth his head"* (1 Cor. 11:4).

My Purpose as a Woman in the Church

The women of the church are guardians of the two coverings.

Head coverings are taught in 1 Corinthians 11. The woman who represents man has to have her head covered. The first covering is the long hair, which has been given to her; it is her glory. When we are at a church meeting, only God is to get the glory and our long hair that is our glory, must be covered. God does not share His glory with any one.

My Purpose as a Woman in the Church

The second covering is a hat or veil to be put over the hair (her glory is to be hidden). Because the woman represents the man, he is not to be glorified. Remember that God's glory is to shine forth in an assembly meeting.

Verses 5-16 in 1 Corinthians 11 covers the truths about two coverings that the women are to look after. Some people argue that there is only one covering (the hair). If that were the case the man would have to take off his hair.

My Purpose as a Woman in the Church

The women teach the angels about the Headship of Christ. Why do the angels watch us? Angels have been observing Creation right through the ages up until the church. In 1 Peter 1:12 we read,

"...Which things the angels desire to look into."

The woman's glory covered is a symbol of authority and the angels looking down out of heaven are taught that there are people on the earth who give God the glory and show that God still has control over the earth.

My Purpose as a Woman in the Church

One of the most important things that we can do as women is to pray:

Pray for:

1. Gospel outreach;
2. Sunday school-pupils for salvation & for the teachers;
3. Go through your church contact list and pray for the needs of the believers and missionaries who are sometimes forgotten.
4. Also pray for your elders who shepherd over you.

May 23

My Purpose as a Woman in the Church

There are practical jobs around the assembly:

1. Helping in the kitchen, bringing food for planned activities.
2. Help in serving and cleaning up.
3. Water plants.
4. Decorating for special occasions: weddings, funerals, and graduations, etc.
5. Making curtains or tablecloths that need replacing.
6. Looking after kitchen and bathroom supplies.

"He (she) *that is faithful in that which is least is faithful also in much"* (Luke 16:10).

My Purpose as a Woman in the Church

In Romans 12:13 we are encouraged to look after the needs of the saints and to give hospitality. *"Distributing to the necessity of saints; given to hospitality."* Women do this better than men.

Hospitality can be shown to:

1. A man or woman who has just lost their spouse.
2. Visitors from out of town.
3. Elderly people who feel very much alone.
4. Students from out of town.

Always remember the single people in your group; they should be included with couples.

My Purpose as a Woman in the Church

As a woman you are more in tune with the needs of those that are hurting. We need to grace our assemblies with kindness.

Phoebe was a servant of the church and a great help to many people.

> *"...she has been a succourer of many, and of myself also"*
> (Rom. 16: 1,2).

We need to do good to all men, but especially to all true believers.

> *"... especially unto them who are of the household of faith."*
> (Gal. 6:10).

My Purpose as a Woman in the Church

As a woman in the church we are to exercise our gift or gifts to edify the Church and to glorify God.

In Romans 12:3-8 we have the concept of the human body. Every member of the body is needed. The little finger is as needed as the nose. God gives us gifts to build up His church.

We need to dedicate our gifts to God's service and not for our own personal use.

My Purpose as a Woman in the Church

In 1 Corinthians 12:27-31 we have a selection of gifts given to the church. Some of these gifts have passed away because we have the whole canon of scripture now. Check out chapter 13:8.

Gifts are good only if ministered in love (1 Cor. 13:1,2).

They are certain areas where woman excel over the man, such as our influence on the family, hospitality and teaching younger women.

My Purpose as a Woman in the Church

The gift of serving or help—Lydia (Acts 16:14-15):

1. Opening your home to visitors.
2. Helping with potluck dinners, etc.
3. Writing notes, sending cards to people who need encouragement.
4. Praying for each member of the assembly.
5. Some women develop ministries: young mothers, unwed mothers, clothing distribution or just women in need.

Lydia's words were, *"come into my house, and abide there."*

My Purpose as a Woman in the Church

The gift of giving—Dorcas (Acts 9:36-39):

1. These women find people in their neighbourhood who need things.
2. There is giving to missions.
3. Giving of our time to soup kitchens.

There were women in Luke 8:1-3 who gave of their substance to the Lord while He was preaching about the Kingdom of God through out the cities and villages.

_____
_____
_____
_____
_____
_____

My Purpose as a Woman in the Church

The gift of encouragement—(Titus 2:1-5):

The aged women were to encourage or train the younger women to be good wives and mothers by their example. The encouraging involved teaching, as well as motivating others to walk with the Lord.

We can build friendships by calling someone who is missing from our meetings for awhile or visiting them. We can encourage children, husbands, elders and deacons.

My Purpose as a Woman in the Church

The gift of mercy—(Rom. 12:8):

"He that shows mercy, with cheerfulness." This gift involves compassion, sympathy, patience and understanding.

The people who need mercy are the depressed, the poor, the orphan, and the bereaved, to name just a few. Showing mercy should be characteristic of all believers, but some Christians excel in this area and open up their hearts and homes for all those who are weary and burdened with life.

My Purpose as a Woman

Those who have the gift of leadership or administration probably already know what areas they are good in. Some examples include:

1. Starting a church library.
2. Organizing conference meals or potluck dinners.
3. Arranging camps for girls, looking after registration and accommodations.
4. Organizing ladies' retreat, showers, etc.
5. Organizing hot meals for the sick, a shepherding program for the aged, a hospitality program.

Every ministry needs organizing.

My Purpose as a Woman

Gift of a teacher —Pricilla (Acts 18:24-26):

> *"....whom when Aquila and Priscilla had heard they took him unto them, and expounded* [taught] *unto him the way of God more perfectly."*

Eunice, in 2 Timothy 1:5, taught Timothy, a child.

We can teach our children, a Sunday school class or a ladies' Bible study. We must make sure that what we are teaching corresponds with what the ladies would like, and that our life matches with what we teach.

My Purpose as a Woman

With the gift of teaching, the older women are to instruct the younger by words and by example.

> *"The aged women likewise, that they be in behaviour as becometh holiness, not false accuser, not give to much wine, teachers of good things; that they may teach the young women to be sober, to love their husbands, to love their children, to be discreet, chaste, keepers at home, good, obedient to their own husbands, that the word of God be not blasphemed"* (Titus 2:3-5).

My Purpose as a Woman

The gift of teaching involves mature women having classes for younger women concerning: family life, child training, and doctrine. This gift may also be seen in women who counsel teenagers or young wives about to be married. Ladies conference speaker.

My Purpose as a Woman

The gift of an evangelist:

The first woman evangelist was the woman at the well. *"Come, see a man, which told me all things that ever I did; is not this the Christ"* (John 4:29).

The evangelist has the ability to clearly present the Gospel, urging men and women to trust Christ now. Two other evangelists at Paul's side in the preaching of the gospel were Euodia and Syntyche (Phil 4:1-2).

As Christians we are all to witness. We could take a neighbourhood Bible study or make up tract of our own to give out.

My Purpose as a Woman

The work of an evangelist might involve:

Starting children's Bible club after school.

Getting involved in international student ministries.

Leading your own children to the Lord is the most wonderful thing a woman can do. When a woman is called of God to preach the gospel she is to be separated unto the Gospel. (Rom. 1:1). Every ambition is nipped in the bud, every desire of life quenched, save only one thing—being separated unto the gospel.

My Purpose as a Woman

To worship the Lord, is the Christian's highest occupation. The highest form of worship is to speak to God about the excellencies of His own dear Son.

"This is My beloved Son, in whom I am well pleased; hear ye Him" (Matt. 17:5).

Worship is the overflowing of the heart occupied with God Himself and with the blessings that God gives us.

My Purpose as a Woman

Worship of the Lord is remembering His death, burial and resurrection. The work of the Lord, which we do for Him, must be guided by the Word of God.

In John 4:23 God expressed His desire for worshippers. We can worship privately, and when the church meets together.

> *"But the hour comes, and now is, when the true worshippers shall worship the Father in spirit and in truth: for the Father seeks such to worship Him."*

Worship before service!!

My Purpose as a Woman

Mary of Bethany was a true worshipper (John 12:1-7), and a silent worshipper! She did not come to hear a sermon, or to make a request, or to meet with the believers, but to refresh the Lord and to fill His heart with joy.

Mary did not withhold her best. Her gift was a costly one. Her life was wholly consecrated to Him.

"Then said Jesus 'Let her alone: against the day of my burying hath she kept this'" (John 12:7).

My Purpose as a Woman

In the New Testament, the Lord's Supper (Acts 2:42), should be prominent where we worship and remember God's Son, Jesus Christ. The Holy Spirit in our hearts will direct our worship. We are to celebrate this precious act of worship until the Lord comes (1 Cor. 11:23-26).

"Ye are my friends, if ye do whatsoever I command you" (John 15:14).

If we want to be called His friend, then we will perform this command.

My Purpose as a Woman

Two essentials for worship are:

1. The Word of God in our hands
2. The Spirit of God in our hearts.

Each person should be free to worship God according to the dictates of his own conscience, as it is enlightened by the revelation God has given in the Holy Scriptures. We are to worship the Father *"the true worshippers shall worship the Father"* (John 4:23) and worship the Son (Phil. 2:10,11).

My Purpose as a Woman

We can worship the Lord by considering the following passages found in Matthew 26-28, Mark 14-16, Luke 22-24, and John 18-20. These chapters give us the details of the crucifixion.

Read Isaiah 50, Psalm 22, Psalm 40 or Psalm 69. These passages are prophecies and anticipate the suffering through which the Lord Jesus passed. Let us meditate on these scriptures, and remember God wants to hear about His Son when we worship the Lord.

My Purpose as a Woman

*"And God said, Let us make man in our image, after our likeness: and let **them** have dominion over..."* (Gen. 1:26).

God put man and woman on equal footing relative to their duties of authority towards the rest of creation.

June 14

My Purpose as a Woman

"And the Lord God said, 'It is not good that the man should be alone; I will make him an helpmeet for him'" (Gen. 2:18).

God made woman for the man and not man for the woman. The woman is to be a help like the man, in same rank of beings, to be near him, cohabit with him and to be always at hand.

My Purpose as a Wife

The man and woman become one in the reproduction act (Genesis 1:28). Just as man is incomplete without the woman, Christ who is the head of the church is not complete without the body which is the Church, His Bride (Eph. 1:22-23).

> *"Therefore shall a man leave his father and his mother, and shall cleave unto his wife: and they shall be one flesh"* (Gen. 2:24).

When we become one in marriage we make a new unit that compliments both of us. Leave what our parents did behind, unless it suits both husband and wife.

My Purpose as a Wife

"And they were both naked, the man and his wife, and were not ashamed" (Gen. 2:25).

The nakedness of the woman is here considered to be natural and normal, and within every marriage relationship it ought to be this way. There should be no shame in the marriage bed in being exposed to one another. We are to have spiritual, intellectual, physical and emotional openness with each other.

My Purpose as a Woman

Knowing we are like God and share His characteristics and emotions gives us self worth (Gen. 1:26). If we downgrade ourselves, we are criticizing what God has made.

Remember that the Son of God confined Himself to a woman's womb and was dependent on her for care and nurture. That one event alone restored women's status.

My Purpose as a Wife

Because Eve was deceived by Satan, and ignored the Lord's warning, the Lord said,

> *"Unto the woman he said, I will greatly multiply thy sorrow and thy conception; in sorrow you shall bring forth children; and thy desire shall be to the husband and he shall rule over you"* (Gen. 3:16).

In the New Testament the dependence of the wife is now to be governed by the sacrificial love of the husband (Eph. 5:25, 28) and not by the whims of a sinful, selfish, self-centered man.

My Purpose as a Wife

"Wives submit yourselves unto your own husbands, as unto the Lord" (Eph. 5:22).

A wise woman will not try to undermine her husband's leadership in the home. She will not use the power of sex to get around him and to get her own way.

We are to submit to each other. We are not to be a doormat. The wife will be willing to let her husband lead when there is a dead lock. This brings harmony and unity into the family.

Strive for unity!

My Purpose as a Woman

"In all thy ways acknowledge Him and he will direct your path" (Prov. 3:6).

How do we acknowledge God? By obeying the Lord! 1 Samuel 15:22 says, *"Behold to obey is better than sacrifice."*

Some women want to do great things for the Lord, but they disregard certain passages of scripture and do not hold them as important to the Lord.

"If you love me, keep my commandments" (John 14:15).

My Purpose as a Woman

We can acknowledge the Lord by demonstrating our trust in Him. Worry is a curse to many women. It robs us of time, and our dependence upon the Lord Himself. He has told us *"Casting all your care upon Him; for He cares for you"* (1 Pet. 5:7).

When we submit to Him. We give up our desires in favour of God's desires. God wants us to offer ourselves as living sacrifices—each day laying our desires aside to follow Him (Rom. 12:1).

June 22

My Purpose as a Woman

We acknowledge the Lord by prayer.

The woman who trusts God and is submissive to Him recognizes her need for divine help and guidance in making decisions.

> *"If any of you lack wisdom, let him ask of God, that gives to all men liberally, and upbraideth not; and it shall be given him"* (Jas. 1:5).

If we need wisdom, we can pray to God and He will supply what we need.

My Purpose as a Woman

The basis for being a godly woman is yielding to God. As a result of this yielding, she becomes like Christ in her life.

"Who can find a virtuous woman? For her price is far above rubies" (Prov. 31:10).

Virtue means the disposition to conform to the law of right, or abstinence from immorality. This women is chaste (sexual purity, pure in thought and in style).

My Purpose as a Wife

"I am only a housewife." How many times have we heard that one?

In Proverbs 31 the housewife is an importer, manager, realtor, seamstress, merchant, etc. Today she has to be a chauffeur, computer expert, cook, maid and gardener.

She works with her hands, gets up early, is careful with money and cares for her family. The hardest job that a woman can do is to look after others and to keep her husband happy.

My Purpose as a Wife

As a woman our basic female trait is found in Ecclesiastes 7:26 *"...whose heart is snares and nets, and her hands as bands."*

Apart from the grace, and mercy of our Lord Jesus Christ our nature tends us toward scheming, plotting, conniving, and using our sexual self to get what we what. We have to relinquish this quest for power by reverencing our husbands.

My Purpose as a Wife

If we do not submit to our Lord, how can we submit to our husbands?

> *"Wives, fit in with your husbands' plans; for then if they refuse to listen when you talk to them about the Lord, they will be won by your respectful, pure behaviour. Your godly lives will speak to them better than any words"* (1 Pet. 3:1-2).

My Purpose as a Wife

We need to develop our inner beauty rather than our outward appearance, winning our husband with love rather than beauty (which can fade away).

> *"Don't be concerned about the outward beauty that depends on jewelry, or stylish clothes or hair arrangements"* (1 Pet. 3:3).

June 28

My Purpose as a Wife

We have our own personalities and we should be ourselves, but the scriptures teach us to have a *"gentle and quiet spirit."*

This quiet spirit makes us teachable. It is an attitude of the heart. It teaches us when to be silent and when to speak.

This gentle spirit is precious to God (1 Pet. 3:4).

"...man looks at the outward appearance but the Lord looks at the heart" 1 Samuel 16:7.

My Purpose as a Wife

The first year of marriage is hard for the woman. She leaves her father's care and then is in the care of her husband (Gen. 2:24). There may be many tears. The Bible speaks of a new wife:

> *"When a man has taken a new wife, he shall not go out to war, neither shall he be charged with any business; but he shall be free at home one year, and shall cheer up his wife which he has taken"* (Deut. 24:5).

So you can see that God knew that young brides would be very emotional!

My Purpose as a Wife

As a wife we are to build up our husband. We don't need to build up his ego or pride but to build his self-confidence in the Lord. We must never take over the household because God intended the husband as the head of the home.

"For the husband is the head of the wife, even as Christ is the head of the church..." (Eph. 5:23).

My Purpose as a Wife

We need to encourage our husbands. Men need an overdose of encouragement—ask for his opinion, ask about his job, and compliment him on it. Appreciate his ideas, and look for his good qualities and not for his weaknesses.

Do not criticize your husband in front of others, especially the children!

My Purpose as a Wife

A wife must pray for her husband and be specific.

A godly wife must not refuse her husband's physical love.

> *"Defraud ye not one the other, except it be with consent for a time, that ye may give yourselves to fasting and prayer; and come together again, that Satan tempt you not for your incontinency"* (1 Cor. 7:5).

We must never be resentful of the time our husbands spend with God.

My Purpose as a Wife

Men desire sexual compatibility. A husband wants a wife who is responsive. If we have a problem with this we can turn to the Scriptures and find the mind of God about sex.

> *"Let thy fountain be blessed: and rejoice with the wife of they youth. Let her be as the loving hind and pleasant roe; let her breasts satisfy thee at all times; and be thou ravished always with her love"* (Prov. 5:18-19).

With a husband, sex is #1 on his list and if he does not get it, he feels that he has no marriage.

He will resent anything that stands in the way!

My Purpose as a Wife

"The heart of her husband does safely trust in her... She will do him good and not evil all the days of her life" (Prov. 31:11-12).

Loyalty is a big item with the husband. One of the most destructive forms of disloyalty is when the wife belittles her husband in front of his children.

The wife who is loyal will not let the relatives pick flaws in him.

And of course there is sexual faithfulness. Marriage is honourable. We must honour our marriage and its vows, and be pure.

My Purpose as a Wife

A wife needs to accept her husband as he is. Acceptance is probably the greatest gift we can give our husbands. We don't try to make our husbands over. The husband should be able to fall flat on his face and we accept him with unconditional love. That also applies to our children. We need to show grace in our families.

July 6

My Purpose as a Wife

A wife needs to allow her husband to be able to express his needs; his fears, his ideas and his hurts without making fun of him. We cannot always solve his problems, but we can listen to them attentively.

"Confess your faults one to another, and pray one for another, that ye may be healed" (Jas. 5:16).

My Purpose as a Wife

Today young women are brought up to be self-reliant, independent and self-sufficient and that is okay up to a point. We have to remember the Bible teaches that the husband has to be the leader in the home but as husband and wife we both have the responsibility of the home, our security and our future together.

July 8

My Purpose as a Wife

A husband and wife need to be partners together—to share. As partners together in Christ we discuss problems, the matters of running the home and we decide together what is best for the home. But if there is a difference of opinion and a deadlock, let the husband have the final decision and let him shoulder the responsibility of that decision.

You are *"heirs together of the grace of life; that your prayers be not hindered"* (1 Pet. 3:7).

My Purpose as a Wife

A wife must make time to enjoy her husband. Remember the children will leave home someday and if we neglect enjoying things with our husband, we will be like strangers. Remember the best gift we can give our child is to look after our marriage partner.

"Every wise woman buildeth her house..." (Prov. 14:1).

My Purpose as a Wife

We are told to love our husbands and we have to make time for him even if it means locking the bedroom door and telling the children, "Don't call me unless the house is on fire!" Make the effort!

There is an adjustment to being a wife and then a mother. Some young women have a hard time with this. Just remember we are first a wife to our husband and then a mother to our children. We can be both! We are to have fun with our husbands. Proverbs 5: 18, 19: *"... rejoice with the wife of thy youth..."*

My Purpose as a Woman

Marriage is God's idea. Man leaves his father and mother and promises himself to his wife.

> *"Whoso finds a wife finds a good thing, and obtaineth favour of the Lord"* (Prov. 18:22).

Strong marriages produce happy children and are the backbone of a healthy nation.

Never be a concubine (common law partner). This is prevalent to day but it is not God's way, and it is living in sin.

My Purpose as a Woman

God brought the woman to the man.

Eve—Adam

Rebekah—Isaac

Rachel—Jacob etc.

This is a principle that should be well taken, not the woman chasing the man.

> *"And the rib, which the Lord God had taken from man, made he a woman, and brought her unto the man"* (Gen. 2:22).

My Purpose as a Wife

To have a strong marriage we must be committed. We are a "throw-it-away" society today, and sad to say this seems to include marriage.

We must never threaten to leave. Marriage and family are top priority. We stick together through thick and thin. We stand up for each other. We face good times and bad times together.

Love *"Bears all things, believes all things, hopes all things, endures all things"* (1 Cor. 13:14). This is commitment!

My Purpose as a Wife

Hints for making your husband happy:

1. Be prepared to give your marriage 100%.
2. Try to run the household smoothly.
3. Keep yourself neat and tidy.
4. Keep a sense of humour.
5. Adapt your schedule to his.
6. Be a good listener.
7. When he enters the house don't immediately load him with troubles.
8. Don't keep him waiting.
9. Keep the children under control and quiet.

My Purpose as a Wife

After years of making meals I learned a few things, such as:

1. Plan menus for the week.
2. When you make a new recipe ask your husband if he likes it, if he doesn't like it—sack it.
3. Enjoy the foods of the season. Try different recipes for each new fruit or vegetable.
4. Shop with a list. There is nothing more tiring than forgetting an item.
5. Whatever you do, don't take the children along or go shopping when you are hungry (Prov. 31:14).

My Purpose as a Wife

Proverbs 12:4 states: *"A virtuous woman is a crown to her husband: but she that maketh ashamed is as rottenness in his bones"* (It corrodes and tears down his strength).

A good woman that is pious and prudent, looks to the good of her family and is conscious of her duty. She is like a crown to her husband. A crown is an ensign of power. She is submissive and faithful to him and by her example she teaches his children to honour their father.

My Purpose as a Wife

"Every wise woman builds her house: but the foolish plucks it down with her hands" (Prov. 14:1).

A wise woman not only builds her house with love but she pays the bills, brings in provisions, and runs the household. She makes sure the children are well educated and looks after their health.

_____

_____

_____

_____

_____

_____

My Purpose as a Wife

Proverbs 19:13 instructs wives not to nag. A wife who is nagging must stop it! It does not work.

> *"A foolish son is the calamity of his father: and the contentions of a wife are a continual dropping* [dripping faucet].*"*

This includes arguing and wanting to be right all the time. If a couple are always arguing, both want power. The wife must drop her desire to be right and she must submit!

My Purpose as a Wife

The wife in Proverbs 31 is hard to follow because most of us have no hired hands but our own, but we can learn from her. There are many negative things said about women in Proverbs but the last chapter describes the best of women (Prov. 31:10-31).

Proverbs 1:7 starts out with, *"The fear of the Lord is the beginning of knowledge..."* and ends with a woman who attains to this command.

My Purpose as a Wife

The picture of the woman in Proverbs 31 is that she is a commendable wife and mother. She is a real business woman and very industrious. She is one who lives for her family. She has refined tastes, and is disciplined and orderly. She has compassion for the needy. She is spiritually-minded and gives herself to hospitality. Her qualities, when coupled with the fear of God, results in a life of enjoyment, honour and success, and of great personal worth.

My Purpose as a Wife

"The heart of her husband does safely trust in her, so that he shall have no need of spoil" (Prov. 31:11).

The wife who commands and controls her own spirit also knows how to manage other people. She is a great helpmeet for her man. She has good principles and stands firm on them.

July 22

My Purpose as a Wife

A good wife makes it her business to adapt and please her husband, while also remembering that he is a sinner saved by grace. If the husband is unsaved he will feel safe and have confidence in her, knowing that she cares for him above everything else.

"She will do him good and not evil all the days of her life" (Prov. 31:12).

My Purpose as a Wife

Kiss your husband good bye in the morning and in the evening when he comes home. This gives great security and peace for the children to see and to know Mom and Dad are glad to see each other. Our goal should be to meet our husband wearing clean clothes, having the house tidy and neat.

A woman can make a house a home.

My Purpose as a Wife

A good wife will look for bargains. She will also make sure her meals are nutritious. She will see that the children have proper meals, not allowing them raid the fridge any time they desire to do so. She will avoid having junk food in the house.

A good wife arises early and doesn't go around all day in her housecoat. She has a plan of action for the day. She will not stay up all night watching TV and lie in bed until noon.

"She rises also while it is yet night, and gives meat to her household, and a portion to her maidens" (Prov. 31:15).

My Purpose as a Wife

"She considers a field, and buys it: with the fruit of her hands she plants a vineyard. She is energetic and a hard worker. She watches out for bargains and that her merchandise is good: and she works far into the night" (Prov. 31:16-19).

She has a plan of action for that day. If the lawn has to be cut or gardening has to be done, she is right in there doing it.

My Purpose as a Wife

The husband and wife are to be submissive to each other. It is a 100% relationship, not 50-50.

They are to have a mutual relationship of unity and equality and behave toward each other in love and grace. They are to be subject one to another out of love and reverence for Christ.

"That you may with one mind and one mouth glorify God, even the Father of our Lord Jesus Christ" (Rom. 15:6).

My Purpose as a Wife

Having different roles in the family does not affect equality. Equality will lead wives and husbands to meet each other's emotional, spiritual and physical needs. This helps each one to accomplish personal fulfillment.

A wife does not surrender her personality to her husband. When the wife does this she has less to give to the relationship. A wife who loses herself might become hostile, feeling trapped. This will lead to separate lives.

My Purpose as a Wife

If a husband and wife have to make a decision for the family, both will want to seek divine leadership in this matter. They can pray together or pray separately, for God's leadership.

Both need to know God's will in the Bible and know the needs of the other and what is right for their partner.

My Purpose as a Woman

The man cannot be alone. He and the woman represent or reflect the image of God.

In Galatians 3:28 we are equal in God's sight.

> *"There is neither Jew nor Greek, there is neither bond nor free, there is neither male nor female: for you are all one in Christ Jesus."*

This is on the grounds of the finished work of Christ.

My Purpose as a Woman

We need discernment when dealing with our husband and children or other believers.

"She opens her mouth with wisdom: and in her tongue is the law of kindness" (Prov. 31:26).

One of the most important things in your life is to have a good attitude, especially when there is many crosses to bear; disappointing grown children, nasty relatives and the list goes on—but you can have a good attitude!

My Purpose as a Woman

In the Song of Solomon 7:10 it says: *"I am my beloved's, and his desire is toward me."*

If you are discouraged about your life or husband, the woman in this verse has comfort by the grace of God because the same desire that tied her to the husband now ties her to the heart of the Bridegroom, which is Christ. His desire is focused upon her and her alone.

My Purpose as a Wife

There is a phrase in the New Testament used for the edification of believers, but can be related to marriage and it is *"One another."* This phrase would be a good study especially to learn to love our fellow believers, but try it in our marriages as well to learn to love our husbands more.

My Purpose as a Wife

I found out from my teenage daughters that girls after the age of 13 rarely get any affection from their parents: no hugs or kisses. Being affectionate in the marriage is a good habit. Do you give an unexpected hug to your husband and children?

"Be kindly affectionate one to another with brotherly love; in honour preferring one another" (Rom. 12:10).

My Purpose as a Wife

Do you send little love letters in your husband's lunch?

Do you tell him how much you love him?

Love is the most important factor in this life. Express this love by doing special things for him. When he has a highlight in his life, how about sending him flowers to his office or work. Maybe it would be a good time when he feels low—make it a mushy card!

> *"...but to love one another: for he that loveth another hath fulfilled the law"* (Rom. 13:8).

My Purpose as a Wife

Do your eyes light up when your husband comes in the room? Do you focus on him or just keep on doing what you were doing when he comes in to the house?

"Greet ye one another with an holy kiss." (1 Cor. 16:20).

In the marriage, make this one a passionate kiss!

My Purpose as a Wife

It is shocking today how many wives and husbands want to control the other partner. A lot of women want to make over the man. To have harmony in the home we need to be blind to our partner's faults and to build each other up.

On the fridge door we should put up a sign: **No negative talk in this house!**

> *"Let us therefore follow after the things which make for peace, and things wherewith one may edify another"* (Rom. 14:19).

My Purpose as a Wife

When a husband gets annoyed or says things that hurt—do not retaliate! Answer with positive and kindly words (a little honey will do). About 90% of the frictions of every day life come from the tone of our voices. Think how Christ would answer. To talk kindly and firmly calms the husband down but wild words will start a fight.

Read Philippians 2:1-4 to find out Christ's attitude to everyday problems.

> *"Now the God of patience and consolation grant you to be like-minded one toward another according to Christ Jesus"* (Rom. 15:5).

My Purpose as a Wife

In Romans 15:14 it says we are to *"admonish one another."* The word admonish means to administer mild reproof. We must never admonish our husbands in public but if it is done in private please leave him his dignity, and do it with love (this can apply to your children too). Don't bring up past faults. Men have very fragile egos and they take rejection hard — so we must pray before we do this.

My Purpose as a Wife

1 Corinthians 11:33 encourages us that *"when we come together to eat, wait one for another."* This could apply to our own daily lives especially at the dinner table when the family gathers together. It should be a pleasant, informative communication and end the meal with prayer and the reading of the Bible.

Many families do not eat together; everybody is out doing their own thing.

My Purpose as a Wife

Some women only care if they are right and they always have to be right. Wives and husbands who are more interested in their rights than in pleasing each other, wind up with all their rights and no one to share their life with. Do not keep an account or keep track of past misdemeanors.

> *"That there should be no schism in the body:* (the church) *but that the members should have the same care one for another"* (1 Cor. 12:25).

<u>_____</u>
<u>_____</u>
<u>_____</u>
<u>_____</u>
<u>_____</u>
<u>_____</u>

My Purpose as a Wife

In Galatians 5:13b we are called to "*...by love serve one another.*"

Christ was the perfect servant. As wives we should not be upset if we need to pick up after our husband, put the toilet seat down, or take out the garbage. If we are motivated by love we will not criticize when the job at hand has been forgotten. Of course a thoughtful husband would do these things.

My Purpose as a Wife

"Bear ye one another's burdens, and so fulfill the law of Christ" (Gal. 6:2).

Sometimes husbands don't want to burden the wife with their problems, but that is why God created the woman for the man—to share his burdens. We may have to work on our husbands to talk about their burdens. Ask for God's help on how to approach the husband in this area of marriage.

My Purpose as a Wife

Before marriage many girls dream of how their husband should be in the marriage, only to learn he is far from perfect. So we must with help from the Lord accept and love our husband, in spite of his faults. We need patience and a gentle spirit in dealing with our partners.

> *"With all lowliness and meekness, with longsuffering, forbearing one another in love"* (Eph. 4:2).

My Purpose as a Wife

"Forbearing one another, and forgiving one another, if any man have a quarrel against any: even as Christ forgave you, so also do ye" (Col. 3:13).

Forbearing one another or forgiving one another comes into play when our partner says some hurtful things. I believe every wife has experienced this and as women we have long memories. The key to forgiving our husbands is to remember that Christ forgave us and we need to do the same with our husbands. It is called "grace."

My Purpose as a Wife

"And be ye kind one to another, tenderhearted, forgiving one another, even as God for Christ's sake hath forgiven you" (Eph. 4:32).

Years ago as a young girl I overheard one man say to another concerning this verse which on a wall plaque and given as a wedding present, "This verse needs to be in every believer's living room. It should be given to all newlyweds." If we exercise kindness with our spouses there will be a difference in our marriages.

My Purpose as a Wife

There will be times when we need to forgive our husband and this should be done right away. Don't dwell on the hurt and coddle it. Don't play the martyr! We cannot have fellowship with God and have our own sins forgiven if we don't forgive. Think of how great it is to make up!

> *"For if ye forgive men their trespasses, your heavenly Father will also forgive you: But if ye forgive not men their trespasses, neither will your Father forgive your trespasses"* (Matt. 6:14,15).

My Purpose as a Wife

I often wonder how much we lie without knowing we are doing it, or the little white lies we may tell our husbands. I shudder as I write this. My prayer each day would be: "God forbid that I should lie to my husband. Please keep my tongue pure and full of truth." We should be dead to lying.

> *"Lie not one to another, seeing that ye have put off the old man with his deeds: and have put on the new man, which is renewed in knowledge after the image of Him that created him"* (Col. 3:9,10).

My Purpose as a Wife

In my own experience, there are some Christian ladies who have confided in me that their husband doesn't love them.

The husband has actually said that to the wife! This is the ultimate hurt! If this is the case, we must keep abounding in love to our husbands. If we are full of God's love we need to keep showing and expressing love regardless of the condition of the husband. Let us ask God to fill us with His never-ending supply of love.

> *"And the Lord make you to increase and abound in love one toward another..."* (1 Thess. 3:12).

My Purpose as a Wife

"Wherefore comfort one another with these words" (1 Thess. 4:18).

This verse applies to the rapture of the church. Some of us Christians are in our "golden years"; but are they golden? As we get older there is a lot of pain, sickness and just plain tiredness, but husband and wife can comfort each other and live for the Lord's return—because we don't really want to see death. The Lord's return is our greatest hope!!

My Purpose as a Wife

As the day of Christ will soon appear, wife and husband need to encourage each other in the Lord's work. Both may lead busy lives but do not begrudge the time your husband spends with the Lord.

> *"And let us consider one another to provoke unto love and to good works…"* (Heb. 10:24).

My Purpose as a Wife

"Speak not evil one of another..." (Jas. 4:11).

One of the first lessons that I remember from my mother is: "If you haven't got anything nice to say, don't bother saying anything at all."

If it is necessary to criticize our husbands, let's make sure we have some friendly advice. A critical spirit can break a spouse's spirit.

My Purpose as a Wife

"Grudge not one against another" (Jas. 5:9).

When life seems to go wrong, we want to blame others for our misfortunes. A husband can be an easy target. Remember Adam and Eve! Adam blamed Eve and Eve blamed the serpent.

Instead let's look inward and take responsibility for our own sinful self and admit our own sin and apologize to God.

My Purpose as a Wife

"Use hospitality one to another without grudging" (1 Pet. 4:9).

This verse applies to the local church, but how many of us ever take our husbands on a date, plan a weekend away, plan a picnic by the fireside on a wintry day? Let's send the children off and have some fun!

My Purpose as a Mother

"Finally, be ye all of one mind, having compassion one of another, love as brethren, be pitiful, be courteous" (1 Pet. 3:8).

This verse applies to the family of God but it can also apply this to our own family life.

Do we encourage the success of our family? Does our family work for the same goals? Are we working for harmony in the home? Do we respond to each other's needs? The world is so cold, are we encouraging hugs and kisses and much affection? Are we teaching our family to be courteous?

My Purpose as a Mother

"Likewise, ye younger, submit yourselves unto the elder..."
(1 Pet. 5:5).

Mother's need to teach their children to respect their elders. This teaching is lacking in our society today. Children do all the talking today. As a child I listened to what my older relatives talked about and I learnt a lot from them and respected them.

My Purpose as a Wife

"And thy desire shall be to thy husband, and he shall rule over thee" (Gen. 3:16b).

The curse of sin came upon the woman and the man. The woman suffers from the dependence on man. Down through the centuries man has dominated the woman. With the power of the gospel, women have found a measure of reprieve from the domination of the man. The man is to love sacrificially (Eph. 5:25).

My Purpose as a Mother

"Unto the woman he said, I will greatly multiply thy sorrow and thy conception, in sorrow you shall bring forth children..." (Gen. 3:16a).

This is the first mention of motherhood.

Eve had been deceived and this was part of her curse. Remember, at Calvary God came down to help the condemned motherhood by Himself being the curse and putting away sin.

He is the sacrifice. The Lord on the cross remembered His mother and made sure she was looked after.

August 27

My Purpose as a Mother

Hannah in 1 Samuel 1 is an example of the purpose of having a family. She prays for a man-child to give back to God. God lends us a child so we can give the child back to Him for His service.

> *"And she was in bitterness of soul, and prayed unto the Lord and wept sore"* (v. 10).

We should pray for our child before it is born for salvation and service to the Lord.

My Purpose as a Mother

It is not easy to bring up children. We are reminded in Isaiah 1:2, *"Hear, O heavens, and give ear, O earth: for the Lord hath spoken, I have nourished and brought up children, and they have rebelled against me."*

If our children are rebelling, let's remember this verse and it should encourage us in our heartache when we contend with a child that is rebelling against us and our counsel.

My Purpose as a Mother

"Train up a child in the way he should go: and when he is old, he will not depart from it" (Prov. 22:6).

As soon as children become adults we have to let them go and hopefully they will choose a path that we have taught them, which is to follow the Lord and He will direct their paths.

My Purpose as a Mother

Our family is our mission field and the work of the Lord. Some Christians who want to serve the Lord neglect their families. Remember Joshua who said, *"As for me and my house we will serve the Lord"* (Josh. 24:15).

This is taking a definite stand for the Lord, which includes our children...

My Purpose as a Mother

Some Christians are fearful to bring up children in such an immoral society, but remember in Exodus 1-2 we have an example of Moses' parents who went ahead and had children in very dark days. Aaron became the high priest, Miriam was a prophetess and Moses was the greatest statesman the world has ever seen.

My Purpose as a Mother

The woman shall have sorrow in child bearing. But when the child is born it is forgotten and then there is great joy or, in my own case, relief!!

"A woman when she is in travail has sorrow, because her hour is come: but as soon as she is delivered of the child, she remembers no more the anguish, for joy that a man [mankind] is born into the world" (John 16:21).

My Purpose as a Mother

Read the book of Proverbs for instructing children in correction and teaching children the ways of the world. This is wisdom from God on how to discipline children but also to show children what is expected out of life. If we are in a bind we must pray for wisdom. The Bible teaches us a lot about life.

"Every wise woman builds her house: but the foolish plucks it down with her hands" (Prov. 14:1).

_____

_____

_____

_____

_____

_____

My Purpose as a Mother

The rod (spanking a child) should be the last resort in disciplining our children. It is wise to break the child's will when he is very young, but do not break the spirit of a child by nagging and threatening him "to death." When we make a threat or a promise we must carry it out.

"He that spares his rod hates his son: but he that loves him disciplines him promptly (early)" (Prov. 13:24).

September 4

My Purpose as a Mother

Those who don't discipline their children show a lack of concern for developing the character of a child. Without discipline children will not know right from wrong.

> *"Chasten thy son while there is hope, and let not thy soul spare for his crying"* (Prov. 19:18).

Do not allow loud crying. Teach the children to cry quietly. When they get loud, there is usually rebellion in that cry.

_____
_____
_____
_____
_____
_____
_____

My Purpose as a Mother

The best thing we can give our children is a good marriage. It makes the children strong and confident and gives great security.

Fighting, nagging, and running down our partner will cause the children to feel uneasy and to worry needlessly. Keep negative attitudes out of the marriage.

> *"Whoso findeth a wife finds a good thing, and obtaineth favour of the Lord"* (Prov. 18:22).

My Purpose as a Mother

"It is better to dwell in a corner of the housetop, than with a brawling woman in a wide house" (Prov. 21:9,19).

"It is better to dwell in the wilderness, than with a contentious and an angry woman."

As a woman who belongs to the Lord, it is not Christ-like to brawl, or to be contentious and angry. It is also a poor example for our children.

My Purpose as a Mother

"Train up a child in the way he should go: and when he is old, he will not depart from it" (Prov. 22:6).

Train them as soldiers who are taught to obey a command.

Train them up, not in the way that they would like to go, but in the way they should go.

Train up a child according to what the child can handle.

September 8

My Purpose as a Mother

Train up a child according to Deuteronomy 6:7.

"And thou shalt teach them diligently unto thy children, and shalt talk of them when thou sittest in thine house, and when thou walkest by the way, and when thou liest down, and when thou risest up."

God's words should be in our hearts. What we learn from the Word we should instill on our children. We must do more than just talk about God's Word; we must live it out in our lives.

_____

_____

_____

_____

_____

_____

_____

My Purpose as a Mother

We should teach the plain truth about God, the laws of God, the goodness and love of God, and His will for our lives.

> *"And that their children, which have not known anything, may hear, and learn to fear the Lord your God..."* (Deut. 31:13).

My Purpose as a Mother

When our children grow up, we hope they will not depart from the good instructions we taught them. Sometimes they do, like Solomon who departed. But even he came back when he realized that the things of this world are all vanity and vexation.

"Vanity of vanities, saith the preacher; all is vanity." (Eccl. 12:8).

Solomon ended up saying: *"Fear God, and keep His commandments; for this is the whole duty of man"* (Eccl. 12:13).

My Purpose as a Mother

"Foolishness is bound in the heart of a child; but the rod of correction shall drive it far from him" (Prov. 22:15).

Rebellion is another word for foolishness. Sin is foolishness and it is in the heart of children right from birth. As parents we must discipline, or train, our children to know the difference between right and wrong.

September 12

My Purpose as a Mother

Our greatest care must be about our children's soul. Correction is grievous to both the child and parent. But when correction is given with wisdom and accompanied with prayer, God's blessing on what he tells us to do with a rebellious child should prevent the child's destruction. *"Let the body smart, so that the spirit be saved in the day of the Lord Jesus"* (1 Cor. 5:5).

Read Proverbs 23:13, 14.

My Purpose as a Mother

We should reprove our children because a child left to himself will one day turn against the mother and be abusive to her with bad language and sometimes physical violence.

"The rod and reproof (scolding) *give wisdom: but a child left to himself bringeth his mother to shame"* (Prov. 29:15).

September 14

My Purpose as a Mother

Our children will tire us out with the constant correction; we may even tire of being a mother. But one day they will say thank you because without the discipline, the high-powered job they have could never be done without that training.

Then we will relax and have a friendship with that child that will extended to the end of our days.

"Correct thy son, and he shall give thee rest; yea, he shall give delight into thy soul" (Prov. 29:17) Amen!!

My Purpose as a Mother

It is not wise to try to be a friend to our children, we must just be a parent. When we are tempted to give up and let them do want they want, because we are scared we will lose their love, remember—this constant discipline will help them to learn to cope with life and make them wise so that they can make good decisions concerning their future.

> *"There is a generation that curseth their father, and doth not bless their mother"* (Prov. 30:11).

Don't give up!

My Purpose as a Mother

It is the duty of a mother to teach her children what is good, that they may do it and what is evil, that they may avoid it. Make this a priority especially when they are young and tender because by the time they become teenagers, their minds will be fashioned to know what is good for them.

It will come into their mind and they will remember.

> *"The words of king Lemuel, the prophecy that his mother taught him"* (Prov. 31:1).

My Purpose as a Mother

We must warn our children against the temptations of drink and drugs when they are young.

> *"It is not for kings, O Lemuel, it is not for kings to drink wine; nor for princes strong drink: Lest they drink, and forget the law, and pervert the judgment of any of the afflicted. Give strong drink unto him that is ready to perish..."* (Prov. 31:4-7).

Drinking might be understandable among unbelievers who are on the verge of dying, but it is not right for leaders of our country who are in power, because it clouds the mind and could lead to poor decisions.

My Purpose as a Mother

We need to instruct our children about purity and to keep themselves for marriage. They must put Christ first and trust God to find a suitable mate for them.

> *"...whatsoever things are true, whatsoever things are honest, whatsoever things are just, whatsoever thing are pure, whatsoever thing are lovely, whatsoever things are of good report; if there be any virtue, and if there be any praise, think* [dwell] *on these things"* (Phil. 4:8).

My Purpose as a Mother

We need to encourage our children in moderation and not to want everything they see on TV or at the stores. Also, be careful of what is put before their eyes. A picture lasts longer than words.

"I will set no wicked thing before mine eyes…" (Ps. 101:3).

September 20

My Purpose as a Mother

Childhood should be a time of discovery, fun, learning and just being a child. Don't encourage dating, at least not until they are sixteen because before that age they cannot handle the over-whelming feelings and passions that comes with dating.

"To everything there is a season, and a time to every purpose under the heaven" (Eccl. 3:1).

My Purpose as a Mother

It seems today, parents want their children to experience all aspects of life right away.

They have to join many activities, and they have no time to be just a child and to play with friends. If this happens when they are so young, what do they have to look forward to when they are older? Don't overwhelm a child with so many regulated lessons.

> *"When I was a child, I spoke as a child, I understood as a child, I though as a child: but when I became a man I put away childish things"* (1 Cor. 13:11).

September 22

My Purpose as a Mother

Bring a child (baby) early to church. The child will watch and will realize the importance of reverence and quietness in the House of God. At home have the child sit on your lap for about 15 minutes as you read them a book or listening to a tape. This is good training!

> *"Gather the people together, men, and women, and children ... that they may hear, and that they may learn, and fear the Lord your God, and observe to do all the words of this law"* (Deut. 31:12).

My Purpose as a Mother

Don't feed a child to keep him quiet. The child can learn to sit still. At the age of fourteen I had a class of preschoolers, 24 of them all in a small Sunday school room. These children were taught at home to be quiet and to speak only when they were spoken too. They were quiet and well behaved. You could not do that today—sad to say!

> *"A wise son maketh a glad father: but a foolish son is the heaviness of his mother"* (Prov. 10:1).

My Purpose as a Mother

A mother can learn to distinguish a cry of hurting from a cry of rebellion. A child who cries long and loud needs to be hushed up right away and taught to cry quietly.

If a baby cries try:

1. Swaddling the baby in a blanket with its arms by its side. (A bit tight)

2. Lying it on its right side and rocking it.

3. Shhhh in its ear until it is quiet. Your womb was the sound of a vacuum cleaner. The baby needs some noise.

Keeping a house quiet is a myth!

My Purpose as a Mother

A child, who has a tantrum or does not obey you in a public place, should be taken home right away and told he will not go out again until he can control him or herself. **Mother, follow through with it.**

Above all we must keep our word. If we promise to spank the child, we must do it! Don't keep threatening. It is called "Tough Love."

When a child is continuously rebelling and is hard to live with, take away something that is precious to the child and give it away. The child will soon learn to behave.

My Purpose as a Mother

A good mother will never call her children "stupid" or any such name.

> *"A soft answer turneth away wrath: but grievous words stir up anger"* (Prov. 15:1).

Remember these words when talking to a teenager or husband. It is hard to argue with a person who is talking softly.

> *"Gentle words cause life and health; griping brings discouragement"* (Prov. 15:4).

My Purpose as a Mother

It is wonderful when children leave home and they are thankful for the discipline they were given. That discipline included dragging them off to church, even when they did not want to go; telling them to go some place that they had committed to, regardless of something that came up that was more exciting, etc. etc.

> *"Her children arise up, and call her blessed; her husband also, and he praiseth her"* (Prov. 31:28).

September 28

My Purpose as a Mother

Our children and their friends will be our mission field. It is a great blessing to see our children saved when they are young. Do not force salvation on them by quoting a prayer for them to follow and repeat. The Holy Spirit will convict them and they will come to us for an explanation of the way of salvation. Just explain and then let them believe and receive Christ on their own (John 1:12).

My Purpose as a Mother

Discipline is for the ultimate good of a child, both in this life and for eternity so is tenderness and compassion.

> *"Like as a father pitieth his children, so the Lord pitieth them that fear him"* (Ps. 103:13).

My daughter's peers rarely got affection, hugs and kisses after the elementary school age. When one of our family comes into a room do our eyes light up at their presence?

My Purpose as a Mother

Children need to be taught to respect authority and to honour their parents and older people.

"Children, obey your parents in the Lord: for this is right. Honour thy father and mother; which is the first commandment with promise; that it may be well with thee, and thou mayest live long on the earth" (Eph. 6:1,2,3).

The obeying is while they are at home but the honouring should be until the parents die. Even after you die, they live by your example.

My Purpose as a Mother

There are some mothers who have to work.

Let's not be pressured by the world to fulfill ourselves or to become a super mom.

The woman in Proverbs did some outside work but she had inside help. We are encouraged in Titus 2:4 to be keepers at home, especially when the children are young.

God will use our children to teach us how to deal with human nature and difficult people—think of it as God's training school.

My Purpose as a Mother

Children need to be shown the reality of God in our lives—not just information about God but they should see God working in our life.

They need to be taught that life is short and then there is eternity. Remember the child is thrown into a world of swearing, crudeness, lying, cheating and no respect for authority.

> *"And, ye fathers, provoke not your children to wrath: but bring them up in the nurture and admonition of he Lord"* (Eph. 6:4).

My Purpose as a Mother

Children should be taught the distinction of the sexes. Satan would like to us to be unisex. Men and women are not to reverse their sexual roles.

> "The woman shall not wear that which pertaineth unto a man neither shall a man put on a woman's garment: for all that do so are abomination unto the Lord thy God" (Deut. 22:5).

It would not hurt to get some books on the differences of boys and girls.

October 4

My Purpose as a Mother

The girls need to be taught modesty and the boys need to be taught to respect their sister. I personally think brothers should never fight with their sister, that means no rough housing. Everyone keeps their hands to themselves. I have seen brothers get real rough with their sisters. I would class this as unseemly behaviour, and it should not allowed in our homes.

"Be kindly affection one to another with brotherly love; in honour preferring one another" Romans 12:10

My Purpose as a Mother

In western society men are taught not to cry or show their feelings, so now we are left with a "macho" man who is hard, callous and very insensitive. Why do you think God made tears? Remember too, *"Jesus wept"* (John 11:25). David is a good type of man—a warrior but he bowed himself, kissed and wept together with Jonathan.

Mothers of sons should read 1 Samuel 16. This gives an outline of how a boy should be brought up.

My Purpose as a Mother

Children should mix with older people so that they can handle themselves later in life. When children have contact only with other children, it limits them in communication with the outside world. The Lord Himself encouraged children around Him. The disciples didn't want to bother with them.

> *"Then were there brought unto Him little children, that He should put His hands on them, and pray and the disciples rebuked them. But Jesus said, 'Suffer little children, and forbid them not, to come unto Me...'"* (Matt. 19:13-14).

Don't be like the disciples.

My Purpose as a Single Gal

A lot of single gals feel tremendous pressure to marry. Sometimes the pressure comes from relatives or friends or they just have a terrible desire to be married. A lot of women think they cannot be complete unless they are married. Both marriage and singleness are good.

> *"...He that is unmarried careth for the things that belong to the Lord, how he may please the Lord: but he that is married careth for the things that are of the world, how he may please his wife"* (1 Cor. 7:33-34).

October 8

My Purpose as a Single Gal

The apostle Paul emphasized that a single person has the opportunity to serve Christ wholeheartedly. Singleness does not guarantee service to God — that takes commitment from the person herself. A single there woman is usually has less responsibility, if she has no family.

> *"There is a difference also between a wife and a virgin. The unmarried woman careth for the things of the Lord, that she may be holy both in body and in spirit: but she that is married careth for the things of the world, how she may please her husband"* (1 Cor. 7:34).

My Purpose as a Single Gal

Lydia in Acts 16:13-15 and 40 was a single career woman. She also owned a home which was a "gathering place" for the Lord's people. She gave hospitality to the Lord's servants. She applied to herself the things that were spoken of by Paul and she was a witness to those around her.

A woman needs to have her own nest, with the things she loves around her. Don't keep waiting and hoping and not make a home for yourself.

October 10

My Purpose as a Single Gal

Mary and Martha were single. Martha was a take-charge type of person and she owned her own home and gave hospitality. Mary was a student of the Lord and sat at his feet.

> *"Now it came to pass, as they went, that He entered into a certain village: and a certain woman named Martha received Him into her house. And she had a sister called Mary, which also sat at Jesus' feet, and heard His Word"* (Luke 10:38-39).

My Purpose as a Single Gal

There was Dorcas who was single and she used her talent with a sewing needle to make clothes for the needy. It was through her there was a revival at Joppa. She took an interest in the widows (Maybe she had been widowed too). Whatever gift you have, use it for the Lord.

Read Act 9:36-42 to find out what a woman she was for the Lord and the reputation she had.

She was well loved!!

October 12

My Purpose as a Single Gal

A young single gal can teach Sunday school, kid's clubs, help at Bible camps, take an interest in a missionary daughter of her own age and write to her. I would encourage single women to support the local assembly and be at the Bible and prayer meetings. (They are not just for old folks you know!)

> *"...I commend you to God, and to the word of his grace, which is able to build you up, and to give you an inheritance among all them which are sanctified"* (Acts 20:32).

My Purpose as a Single Gal

A woman who is contemplating going to college or university: should ask for the Lord's guidance, remembering that these establishments are often anti-Christian. A believer will want to emerge from them a victorious Christian. There will probably be a Christian club on campus.

"And what concord hath Christ with Belial? Or what part hath he that believeth with an infidel?" (2 Cor. 6:15).

My Purpose as a Single Gal

Before going to college, pray over the courses selected. Are they anti-God? It is best to seek out other believers. A godly young woman will want to keep herself pure and keep in the word of God. She must pray consistently that God will keep her from the pollution of godless philosophers and preserve her testimony.

> *"Wherefore come out from among them, and be ye separate, saith the Lord, and touch not the unclean thing; and I will receive you"* (2 Cor. 6:17).

My Purpose as a Single Gal

A popular phrase in our Christian community is: "What Would Jesus Do?" and while we are looking and waiting for the Lord's return, maybe we should have a phrase "What will Jesus find me doing?"

We need to think carefully about the things we are going to do, the places where we go and the things we say and do. We also should be careful of what friends we choose even when they are professing Christians.

> *"Comfort your hearts, and establish you in every good word and work"* (2 Thess. 2:17).

My Purpose as a Single Gal

When a young woman meets a young man and they have serious intentions she should consider:

1. What is his relationship to Jesus Christ? Is he saved/born again?
2. Is he active in a Bible believing church?
3. How does he treat his mother? If he treats her with no respect, he will do the same to you.
4. Does he treat you like a lady or is he more interested in promoting himself?
5. Does he care about your interests and talents?
6. Is he ready to love you as Christ loved the church and gave himself for it?

My Purpose as a Single Parent

I was a single parent for 13 years. I found out that even Christians are prejudiced about a single mother. "She hasn't a husband so the children won't be disciplined." I also found out that some wives lean on their husbands for everything and not the Lord, but some day the husband might not be around so you need to lean on the Lord as your protector. I claimed Isaiah 54:5,6 for myself.

> *"For the Maker is thine husband; the Lord of Hosts... For the Lord hath called thee as a woman forsaken and grieved in spirit, and a wife of youth, when thou was refused, saith thy God."*

October 18

My Purpose as a Single Parent

A single mother should seek out a godly man or elder who can give counsel, also find an older godly woman that she can relate to and have a girl friend she can spill out her feelings and fears to, but God makes a terrific husband! He can do things that a husband could never do and it is exciting to lean on Him and tell Him all our troubles too. And like David we can rant and rave and cry to Him for help.

"God is refuge and strength, a very present help in trouble" (Ps. 46:1).

My Purpose as a Single Parent

My own personal advice: **Wait on the Lord**.

Do not even think of another relationship or ending the marriage. Some Christian women have ended the marriage and got into a blended family and it is confusion. God is not the author of confusion. We have to give God time to work in the heart of a husband.

> *"Wait on the Lord: be of good courage, and He shall strengthen thine heart: wait, I say, on the Lord"* (Ps. 27:14).

October 20

My Purpose as a Single Parent

As a single parent I waited seven years, and then my husband wanted a divorce. When my children were to leave home after getting an education, I knew I was going to be alone. I asked an elder, concerning remarrying and the elder told me I was the wronged party so I could remarry. But I wanted to make sure so I asked God and one month later my second husband came into my life.

"I waited patiently for the Lord; and he inclined unto me, and heard my cry." (Ps. 40:1).

If God had said no, I would have been content with that.

298

My Purpose as a Single Parent

I never talked badly about my children's father.

Today as adults they include their father in the celebrations of life. When they were young and their father was missing from their life, I tried to make life as normal as possible.

We must not relate our fears and problems to the children — they cannot bear adult things. We can get over this ordeal but children never get over their parents divorcing. I could say, "Why me Lord?" but why not? We will have suffering in this life. 1 Peter 1:7 reminds us of this.

October 22

My Purpose as a Single Parent

We must rule our home with an iron hand, but with velvet gloves on. It is called "tough love." A mother is not to be a friend to her children. Save that for when they leave home.

A single mother should lay out her financial needs to the Lord. Nothing is impossible with God. I did not work outside the home until my children were in their teens.

It is the pits being alone because it feels like it is a couple's world, and we singles don't feel like we fit in, even in some Christian circles. But we can overcome our fear of not fitting in.

"These things I haves spoken unto you, that in me you might have peace. In the world you shall have tribulation: but be of good cheer I have over come the world." John 16:32

My Purpose as an Older Woman

In Titus 2:1-5 there is an emphasis on the foundation of a home, which is taught by the older women of the assembly. She is to exercise a pious reverence for God in decency, decorum in clothing, gestures, looks and speech.

They are not to be false accusers, meaning—

No sowers of discord

No slandering

No backbiting their neighbours

No gossiping

No addictions

October 24

My Purpose as an Older Woman

She is to teach or encourage the young women to be sober which is mark of self-control and sound moral judgment.

"Teaching us that, denying ungodliness and worldly lusts, we should live soberly, righteously, and godly, in this present world" (Titus 2:12).

This helps the young woman to always be alert and to be able to guard against Satan's attack.

My Purpose as an Older Woman

The older woman is to teach younger women doctrinal instruction in a private way.

There is not be any old wives' tales, vain conversations, superstitions, and popular worldly sayings. A younger woman is to be encouraged to love her husband (Where there is true love this will not be difficult to do) and also to obey her husband.

> *"I will therefore that the younger women marry, bear children, guide the house, give none occasion to the adversary to speak reproachfully"* (1 Tim. 5:14).

My Purpose as an Older Woman

She will teach the younger women to love their children, not just a natural affection but also a spiritual love for their souls.

It also means to discipline your children and see to their education, teaching them manners and trying to form their lives and character (before the age of six.)

In Titus 2:5 it says to be discreet which means to be tactful in dealing with others or to be wise.

My Purpose as an Older Woman

She is to teach the younger woman to be chaste.

This word is applied to sexuality, which mean the chaste person is to be innocent of sexual impurity, in desire, imagination, and action.

Also to be keepers at home, not gadding about. The world says you should be fulfilling yourself out in the world, not according to the Word of God.

> *"To be discreet, chaste, keepers at home, good, obedient to their own husbands, that the word of God be not blasphemed"* (Titus 2:5).

Failure in our duties towards God is a reproach to Christianity.

October 28

My Purpose as an Older Woman

In Titus 2:5 we have the word "good."

God Himself is good, Mark 10:18. That means God's works, gifts and commands are good.

Good also means being pleasant, gracious, having a cheerful spirit and temperament. It also means to be good natured and to talk pleasantly, not negatively or bitterly. This builds a house and this pleases the husband. We need to put a sign at our door saying: **No negative talk allowed in this house!**

My Purpose as a Widow

God has a special care for widows, starting in Exodus 22:22: *"Ye shall not afflict any widow, or fatherless child."*

A widow's adversary would be severely punished. In the New Testament the Lord denounced the Pharisees and scribes who devoured widows' houses, yet they lived in grandeur. In Acts 6 the disciples got together and picked seven men to look after the widows, because there were widows who were not being looked after.

My Purpose as a Widow

There is a description of a widow in Lamentations 1:1-2. Jerusalem's downfall and desolation is pictured as a widow.

She becomes a widow, she cries in the night, and her tears are upon her cheeks; she has no one to comfort her. She is lonely and is full of sorrow. She is dependent on others.

God does pay special attention to all widows through the Scriptures. A widow should make a study of how He takes care of the widows and the instructions He gives to them.

My Purpose as a Widow

God looked after a widow in 2 Kings 4:1-7. The widow was in terrible debt. The creditor was going to take her two sons to be slaves, but God met her need through Elisha and we have the miracle of the oil being multiplied. She sold the oil and was out of debt. It certainly strengthened her faith in God.

In Luke 7:11-14 the Lord Jesus had pity on a widow who had only one son and he died and was about to be buried. Jesus brought him back from the dead.

November 1

My Purpose as a Widow

The Lord used widows to provide for His servants. In the Old Testament God used a Gentile widow to look after Elijah the prophet during part of a famine. 1 Kings 17:9-24.

In 1 Timothy 5:10 the widow is mentioned,

> *"Well reported of for good works, if she have brought up children, if she have lodged stranger, if she have washed the saints' feet, if she have relieved the afflicted, if she have diligently followed every good work."*

My Purpose as a Widow

In Luke 2:36-38 we have a widow named Anna who gave her life to serving God and working in the temple. In 1 Timothy 5:5 it says, *"Now she that is a widow indeed, and desolate, trusteth in God, and continueth in supplications and prayers night and day."*

Anna fulfilled this verse and she also spoke of the Lord *"to all them that looked for redemption in Jerusalem."* We too are waiting for the Lord's return (1 Thess. 4:16,17).

November 3

My Purpose as a Widow

The Lord used widows as an example of selfless giving. In Luke 21:1-4 we have a widow who cast in all she had into the treasury.

Most of us Christians want to put in a certain percentage of our money, forgetting it is all the Lord's money and not our own. The Lord admires sacrificial giving and a cheerful giver. This widow set the standard by giving her all.

> *"For all these have of their abundance cast in unto the offerings of God: but she of her penury hath cast in all the living that she had"* (Luke 21:4).

My Purpose as a Widow

The presence of a widow in the church teaches us or reminds us to look out for the weak and to show Christ's love by helping in a practical way.

There are many widows on in the mission field. Widows or older women are the back-bone of the prayer meeting. They are to the church an example by their life of faith in God.

A woman who has a husband depends on him. But a widow truly depends on the Lord. She *"trusteth in God,"* for food and clothing (1 Tim. 5:5).

My Purpose as a Widow

In Genesis 38 we have the first widow. Her name was Tamar and she had a wrong relationship with Judah, her father-in-law. But the grace of God put her in the genealogy of the Lord Jesus in Matthew 1:3,

> *"And Judas* [Judah] *begat Phares and Zara of Thamar* [Tamar]."

We see Judah a Jew and Tamar a Gentile as a foreshadowing the fact that Jews and Gentiles were to share in the blessing of the Gospel. It is hard to believe an incestuous act ended up by being a fruitful race, but God overrules evil to His own good purpose.

My Purpose as a Widow

We can learn from other widows in the Bible: Naomi, Ruth and Orpah.

Naomi is a backslider but she is restored to the Lord. We have Orpah who went back to her kindred, which reminds us we should never look back. Then there is the Gentile widow Ruth who said to Naomi:

> *"Entreat me not to leave thee, or to return from following after thee: for whither thou goes, I will go; and where thou lodgest, I will lodge: thy people shall be my people, and thy God my God"* (Ruth 1:16).

This is a wonderful book and a good study for those who are widowed.

November 7

My Purpose as a Widow

Mary the mother of our Lord seems to be a widow because there is no mention of Joseph after the temple incident in Luke 2. There she stands at the cross with other women and she saw what man heaped upon her son. It is very touching that the Lord who was suffering for our sake thought of his mother and gave her over to the care of John. When we last see her she is at a prayer meeting with the disciples in Acts 1:14.

> *"These all continued with one accord in prayer and sup-plication, with the women, and Mary the mother of Jesus, and with his brethren."*

My Purpose as a Widow

The family of a widow should look after her first, but if she has no one in the world, and she is destitute, the church should take the responsibility of looking after her.

> "If any man or woman that believeth have widows, let them relieve them, and let not the church be charged; that it may relieve them that are widows indeed [meaning truly destitute]" (1 Tim. 5:16).

November 9

My Purpose as a Woman

Have you gone to potlucks and sat around the table and tried to have a conversation with the ones near by you? Then later you have had the same saints in your home and what a difference that made! You actually got to know people better by having them in your home. You no longer just said "Good morning. How are you?"

We know about their children, their past, their hopes and even what ails them.

> *"And they, continuing daily with one accord in the temple, and breaking bread from house to house, did eat their meat with gladness and singleness of heart"* (Acts 2:46).

It is called hospitality!

My Purpose as a Woman

"Let brotherly love continue. Be not forgetful to entertain stranger: for thereby some have entertained angels unawares" (Heb. 13:1,2).

When we invite our sisters and brothers, even the least of them, we are inviting the Lord Jesus Christ into our homes. If we look at this way, it will transform how we look at ministering to God's people. Read Matthew 25:34-36,40 to see how the Lord looked at hospitality.

Pray that God will give us joy in this service for Him.

My Purpose as a Wife

Hospitality is a requirement of an elder or a church shepherd and of course you know who does the cooking etc.

> *"This is a true saying, If a man desire the office of a bishop he desireth a good work. A bishop or [elder] then must be blameless, the husband of one wife, vigilant, sober, of good behaviour, given to hospitality, apt to teach"* (1 Tim. 3:1,2).

The home is one of the most important tools for reaching and caring for people.

My Purpose as a Wife

"Use hospitality one to another without grudging" (1
Pet. 4:9).

Christian hospitality is not an option. It is obedience to God.
Plan a day, and if it is Sunday, prepare on Saturday.

Go through the assembly contact list and plunge right in
and invite those on the list. Invite a neighbour in. Think of certain people who have nowhere to go on Christmas. Use the
same recipes that work for you.

If you are scared how the conversation will go, prepare a list
of questions beforehand. Have fun!

November 13

My Purpose as a Mother

In Judges 13 we have a mother who was told by the angel of the Lord to raise her son to be a Nazerite. He was not to drink wine or strong drink or eat anything unclean, so she didn't either. As mothers we need to show an example of what is right. If we are teaching values to our children we need to exhibit the values first.

My Purpose as a Mother

As a mother we need to live out the convictions each day that are founded in the Word of God. We have to guard our mouths, think what kind of effect our words have on our children, and also the tone of our voice. Sometimes we have to refrain from giving out too much information that would confuse a young child.

"In the multitude of words there wanteth not sin: but he that refraineth his lips is wise" (Prov. 10:19).

November 15

My Purpose as a Woman

Whatever you read, see on TV or listen to the radio, CD's or tapes, does it measure up to God's standard? You are what you think. Don't let your mind feed on the world's garbage. It will only bring you down. In 2 Corinthians 10:5 it says:

"Casting down imaginations, and every high things that exalteth itself against the knowledge of God, and bringing into captivity every thought to the obedience of Christ."

My Purpose as a Woman

If we are always feeding on negative things, we are in a trap and need to be freed from it. We are encouraged from the Word of God to mediate on His word and the Bible speaks of renewal of the mind.

> *"And be not conformed to this world: but be ye transformed by the renewing of your mind, that ye may prove what is that good, and acceptable, and perfect, will of God"* (Rom. 12:2).

November 17

My Purpose as a Woman

We are to have the mind of Christ. If something is entertaining sin—turn it off, walk away from it, turn your eyes away from the offending object.

> *"For who hath known the mind of the Lord, that he may instruct him? But we have the mind of Christ"* (1 Cor. 2:16).

My Purpose as a Mother

The mother has an art in comforting in times of sorrow and pain. God likens Himself to a devoted mother. In Isaiah 66:13 God says: *"As one whom his mother comforteth, so will I comfort you...."* This is a sweet and tender character of God! Do you ever notice men on the TV who always say "Hello Mom" when they have a chance to address someone at home?

November 19

My Purpose as a Mother

A child need both parents but a mother's presence, discipline, counsel, sympathy and even her silence at times are really needed in today's world. The world is a very cold place. If we know of a child who has no mother, we should try to move into his or her life with grace, and to mother that child and give good counsel.

My Purpose as a Mother

I was 20 when my mother died. When I came home from work the house was like a motel—cold, dull and empty. I did become closer to my father but it was not the same having as my mother. I was thankful for the love of my father, and brother but above all I was thankful for the love of God, which helped me endure this empty-ache for my mother. It was comforting to know she was safe in heaven.

My Purpose as a Mother-in-law

In Genesis 2:24 the man was to leave his father and his mother, and cleave unto his wife. We must cut the apron strings and accept our child's spouse. Our children need to talk to their spouse about their problems, not us. Make sure to talk to both of them on the phone. Be friendly with your child's in-laws.

"If it be possible, as much as lieth in you, live peaceably with all men" (Rom. 12:18).

My Purpose as a Wife

I have seen a lot of new wives alienate their husbands from their parents. I know there are husbands out there that are Mummy's boy, but it is heartless for the Mother who raised this man to be suddenly cut off from visiting their grandchildren and their son.

"Therefore to him that knoweth to do good, and doeth it not, to him it is sin" (Jas. 4:17).

My Purpose as a Mother-in-law

Be careful how you "Help" in the new family. "Help" may be taken as interference or it may look like criticism on how they run their house and train their children. Ask the Lord for guidance and read Titus 2:4-5. Your family should see you live these verses out and it will be an example to your daughter-in-law to follow.

My Purpose as a Woman

We are encouraged as woman to wear modest clothing that is not gaudy or costly.

> *"In like manner also, that women adorn themselves in modest apparel, with shamefacedness and sobriety: not with broided hair or gold or pearls, or costly array"* (1 Tim. 2:9).

Are your clothes revealing? Do you look like you are poured into your jeans? Do you dress like Hollywood?

Shamefacedness—means to have respect for the men folk so we don't tempt them with the way we dress.

My Purpose as a Woman

A Christian woman should not be known primarily for her outward adornment.

Modest means orderly, not plain, drab or sloppy because that can be offensive too. We are to be free from vanity, excessive pride, not showy, or gaudy and extreme. Sober implies subdued in colour and manner of dress; to be well balanced.

Good taste means knowing what is suitable for the occasion.

"Whose adorning let it not be that outward adorning of plaiting the hair, and of wearing of gold, or of putting on of apparel" (1 Pet. 3:3).

My Purpose as a Woman

"Unto Adam also and to his wife did the Lord God make coats of skins, and clothed them" (Gen. 3:21).

You can see from this scripture that God provided a real cover up for both of them.

The only parts of the body showing were the face, hands and the legs from the knees down.

The beauty of the woman is seen in her works for the Lord *"But* [which becometh women professing godliness] *with good works"* (1 Tim. 2:10).

November 27

My Purpose as a Woman

"Let the woman learn in silence with all subjection. But I suffer not a woman to teach, or to usurp authority over the man but to be in silence," (1 Tim. 2:11 & 12).

Why?

"For Adam was first formed, then Eve. And Adam was not deceived, but the woman being deceived was in the transgression."

Adam disobeyed but Eve stepped out of her place and took the lead. She also added to the Word of God.

My Purpose as a Woman

In Genesis 3:11-14 Adam sinned and was condemned to labour for his food. Eve sinned and women were to have pain through childbirth. The men are to be the leaders and providers and the women are to be the followers and the homemakers . She is to be the preserver of mankind by giving birth.

> *"Notwithstanding she shall be saved in childbearing, if they continue in faith and charity and holiness with sobriety"* (1 Tim. 2:15).

My Purpose as a Woman

What we wear every day in the garden or house should be different from what we wear when we meet with the King of kings and Lord of lords at our public church meeting, especially when we come to remember the Lord.

Do you dress like you are going on a date with the Lord? Do you really believe you are meeting with the Lord?

He promises to be in our midst.

"For where two or three are gathered together in my name, there am I in the midst of them" (Matt. 18:20).

My Purpose as a Wife

"Likewise, ye wives, be in subjection to your own husband; that, if any obey not the word, they also may without the word be won by the conversation of the wives" (1 Pet. 3:1).

If you have an unconverted husband this verse certainly applies to you. You are not to preach to him. Your conversation should be without malice, envy, jealousy or lying. You show respect to everyone. The husband will not listen to preaching, so you have to live Christ before him.

December 1

My Purpose as a Woman

"But let it be the hidden man of the heart, in that which is not corruptible, even the ornament of a meek and quiet spirit, which is in the sight of God of great price" (1 Pet. 3:4).

The hidden man of the heart is the soul. We are to beautify the inner man and not the body, which is going to perish someday. We should show grace, truth and virtue.

My Purpose as a Woman

The finest ornament a Christian woman can wear, by God's standard, is a meek and quiet spirit. To be meek is to be calm, showing patience, having a gentle disposition; a soft place for a husband to land.

Quiet is to be free from turmoil, excessive activity and vexations. We are not to be loud or brash but to have a gentle and a quiet temperament.

December 3

My Purpose as a Mother

"Little children, keep yourselves from idols" (1 John 5:21).

When there is lack of parental guidance, the child becomes dominant in the home, at school and in the playground. The child becomes an idol of self—the tantrums, being a bully all through life and the growth of a big ego are the result of giving into the child.

My Purpose as a Mother

Self worship in a man leads him into believing he is "always right" which makes him a dominating husband and father. Who wants to live with a bully?

The self-idol in a woman usually projects smothering of a child. This child will never want to leave home. It is a death-blow for the young adolescent to be independent and to be self-reliant. It is both terrible to smother and boss a child to death. Both cases wound a child greatly.

December 5

My Purpose as a Mother

There is the idol of popularity and it seems to seep into everyone's home. You must be cool not a nerd! It means we must conform to what everybody else is doing. It starts early with "But mother, everybody does it." This god tells us what to wear, what to play with, what to eat, drink and what to be. As a parent we must squash this idol with: "In this family we don't do this..." and explain why. Know your scriptures so you can back up your words, if possible.

My Purpose as a Mother

There is the idol of materialism or desire for things. It starts usually at the mall—you see young children who say: "I want that or give me that." We have to have all the latest fashions, gadgets and they have to be the best or a famous name product. This "gimme" attitude brings about idolatry.

You see it on the Dr. Phil show where the wife has to shop the family right into bankruptcy to make her feel good. This god never is satisfied. It makes the husband or father to be a human cash register and drives him to have to work harder and longer so that he is not with his family as he should be.

My Purpose as a Woman

The idol of position is usually a man thing, but we women can be guilty of it too. The woman makes herself look good in the community or heaven forbid in the church. She has to have a big home, well furnished or be the best dressed. It is a god of seeking prominence. At a ladies meeting, etc, her opinions or ideas must be first, or she has done it for a 100 years and won't hand the mantle over to a younger woman to help train her for the future. Position is a god!

My Purpose as a Woman

"A man that hath friends must show himself friendly: and there is a friend that sticketh closer than a brother" (Prov. 18:24).

I believe it is important, for a woman to have a good friend. I have had several. Most men do not like small talk or detail; we women do.

A friend keeps us accountable. Of course we have the Lord and we can talk about everything to Him, that we would not want to discuss with our best friend.

December 9

My Purpose as a Woman

One of the enjoyments of my life is to keep journals. The journals have: notes from sermons, sayings from books, magazines and preachers; thoughts that are all based on scriptural principles, poems, cartoons that show the funny quirks in my marriage and friends.

I make notes of the "Signs of the times"(crazy people and things), and a diary, which shows the history and times of my life which I will pass on to my children.

My Purpose as a Mother

When my children became teenagers, they often stayed overnight with friends or went to camps and conferences. Before they went out the door I would say to them, "Remember who you are and remember to keep your name clean from trouble."

*"A **good** name is rather to be chosen than great riches, and loving favour rather than silver and gold"* (Prov. 22:1).

December 11

My Purpose as a Wife

You often hear the expression today, "I am just a housewife" or "I'm just a mother."

Where would civilization be if the women did not manage the house and never had children? It has been said that the homemaker's job is equal to two outside jobs.

> *"Thy wife shall be as a fruitful vine by the sides of thine house: thy children like olive plants round about thy table"* (Ps. 128:3).

This speaks of a peaceful and a plentiful life.

My Purpose as a Woman

Growing up in Sunday school we learnt about all the great men of the Bible. When I got married and had children I started to study the women of the Bible and all the verses pertaining to women. It is thrilling to know about the women who walked and talked with the Lord. The Lord first revealed himself as the Messiah, not to a man, but a despised adulterous woman (John 4:25, 26).

Even the disciples were shocked that the Lord would be speaking to a woman and one who was of a despised race.

December 13

My Purpose as a Woman

Some women say, "I am only a woman."

I think we might remember that there were women in the Bible who made quite an impact on those they came in contact with.

Esther, in chapter 7, risked her life to plead for her Jewish people and confronted her enemy Haman. She helped save her people. God is not mentioned in this book but we see the providence of God and how God used her to save his precious people.

My Purpose as a Woman

It was Mary of Bethany who had the spiritual discernment to know Christ was going to die and she had an alabaster box of ointment for his burial. She was a silent worshipper.

I believe she sensed the Lord's sorrow that the disciples did not seem to observe. She came to give and not get! Many Christians today meet together and expect to receive some blessing. Not Mary she gave her best to the Lord. Read Mark 14:3-9.

My Purpose as a Woman

It was women who sustained the Lord in His three years of ministry and gave to His work. Mark 15:41 states *"when he was in Galilee, followed him, and ministered unto him."* Also in Luke 8:2,3 *"which ministered unto him of their substance."*

Are we doing this today for the missionary work or for the believers who go out in faith doing the work of the Lord?

My Purpose as a Woman

Except for John, it was the women who stayed at the cross when all the disciples had fled.

"Now there stood by the cross of Jesus his mother, and his mother's sister, Mary the wife of Cleophas, and Mary Magdalene" (John 19:25; Mark 15:40; Matt. 27:55,56).

They also watched where He was laid, and when the Sabbath was past they brought sweet spices to prepare for His body.

December 17

My Purpose as a Woman

In Mark 16 it was Mary Magdalene, and Mary the mother of James and Salome who were first at the tomb and were told by an angel to go and tell the disciples that Jesus Christ rose from the dead, Matthew 28:1-9. In Mark 16:9 it says:

> *"Now when Jesus was risen early the first day of the week, he appeared first to Mary Magdalene, out of whom he had cast seven devils."*

The men might get to the moon first but the women are first at seeing the Creator of the universe being raised from the dead!

Hallelujah! What a Saviour!

My Purpose as a Woman

I often think of Abigail who took the risk of facing three hundred angry, hungry men.

She rode to them on a donkey. I would have used a racehorse. She won David first of all by kind words. She was loyal to her drunken, brutish husband. She had confidence in God to speak to David about his predestined future.

In the Old Testament (1 Sam. 25:1-42) Abigail is an example of a women of discernment and one who was respected by her servants.

My Purpose as a Woman

In the dark days of Judges, when every one was doing his own thing, a woman comes on the scene who was a wife and prophetess and a judge. She was called a mother in Israel and her name was Deborah. She aroused the nation from its despair and lethargy. The sovereignty of God let Deborah rule the nation but in Hebrews 11:32, Barak her general was mentioned among he faithful Old Testament saints. God obviously prefers that men rule, but we can be "Mothers in Israel" in our own church gatherings. Read Judges 4 & 5.

My Purpose as a Woman

In 1 Samuel 1 & 2 we have a remarkable woman named Hannah. She made a vow to the Lord and made the ultimate sacrifice; she lent her child Samuel to the Lord. Poor Hannah was abused by the other wife and probably was given a bad time by the women of the village for not having a child. Even the High Priest thought she was drunk when she prayed and cried unto the Lord for a child. Her song of thanksgiving is equal to the Psalms and resembles the song of Mary in the gospel of Luke 1. She was rewarded with five more children.

God takes a vow very seriously!

December 21

My Purpose as a Woman

*"Through faith also **Sara** herself received strength to conceive seed, and was delivered of a child when she was past age, because she judged him faithful who had promised"* (Heb. 11:11).

Imagine waiting all your life for a child! The line of Kings descended from Sarah, ending with God's anointed one, the Messiah. She was unusually beautiful even at the age of 90.

Her conniving for a son is why the Middle East is such a hot spot today, but despite that God declared her faithful.

My Purpose as a Woman

The heart of a mother for her child is shown in Jochebed (Numbers 26:59). She hid her child from the king of Egypt (Ex. 2:1-3). She had three outstanding children

Moses—who became one of the greatest leaders the world, has ever known.

Aaron—who became Israel's first High Priest.

Miriam—the poetess who led the women in the first song of the Bible.

She took a risk of faith and shows us that we too can take an impossible situation to our heavenly Father, trusting Him for the outcome.

December 23

My Purpose as a Woman

When I get to heaven I would like to meet Mrs. Noah (she was not named). We would class her as being tolerant, an encourager for Noah who preached 120 years with no converts and a very submissive wife!

Just imagine getting on a boat with all those creatures. What a story she will have to tell about her experience on the ark.

My Purpose as a Woman

At Christmas time our thoughts go to the birth of Christ and of course to Mary and Joseph.

We are intrigued by a young country girl, who rejoiced in God her Saviour in the song of praise to the Lord.

We note that she was familiar with the Old Testament scriptures and was well taught. Her faith is great, especially in dealing with the probable outrage at her unmarried state.

While reading the Christmas story, read and mediate on her song (Luke 1:46-55).

My Purpose as a Woman

In Luke 2:34,35 Simeon prophesies to Mary about her future concerning her relationship, with Jesus the Son of God.

> *"Yea, a sword shall pierce through thy own soul also, that the thoughts of many hearts may be revealed."*

1st sword: Luke 2:49

2nd sword: John 2:4

3rd sword Matthew 12:46-50

4th sword John 19:25-27

Mary was subject to Christ as the Son of God.

Our last look at Mary is in Acts 1:14, where she is with the believers at a prayer meeting (no worship of Mary is found in Scripture).

My Purpose as a Woman

The apostle Paul reminds Timothy (his son in the faith) of his faithful grandmother and his mother who instructed him in the study of the scriptures. They showed what an influence they had on Timothy's young life, concerning their faith.

> *"When I call to remembrance the unfeigned* [sincere] *faith that is in thee, which dwelt first in thy grandmother Lois, and thy mother Eunice; and I am persuaded that in thee also"* (2 Tim. 1:5).

It would seem that his mother was a believer, but the father was not (Acts 16:1).

My Purpose as a Woman

We have another famous Deborah who was a nanny for Jacob and Esau and also for Jacob's "young tribe." Her name means "Bee." A bee is constantly active, full of industry and care.

Deborah was loyal and devoted and when she passed away she was deeply mourned (Gen. 24:59, 35:8). I think of all those nannies for famous men in history, like Winston Churchill who loved his Nanny.

Nannies have probably more influence on the children they care for than the children's own parents. Some nannies have led very lonely lives, cut off from their families.

My Purpose as a Woman

In the Scriptures we can also learn from other people's tragedies, like Dinah in Genesis 34. She was the daughter of Jacob and Leah. It is a lesson how believers should live a separated life and not follow unbelievers. Dinah is curious about the oriental life of her idolatrous neighbours, girls of her age. She wanted to observe their customs and she sought out their company. Her discontent ended in a terrible massacre of the men who were of the household of her husband-to-be.

My Purpose as a Woman

Think of the queens of England named Elizabeth. This name became famous throughout history. Our own Queen Elizabeth has tried to live her life beyond reproach. Duty was the strong point of her life.

We have an Elizabeth in Luke 1 whose linage was of the High Priest Aaron. She became the mother of John the Baptist, the forerunner of Jesus Christ. Luke 1:5-80 tells a portion of her life. It was her Spirit-filled greeting which prompted Mary to reply in her famous song about the Lord God Almighty.

My Purpose as a Woman

In 2 Kings 11:1-2 we have a princess who married a high priest. She was a very courageous woman who kidnapped her nephew, Joash, from among the corpses of the King's sons and hid him for six years from the murderess, Athaliah. She is credited for preserving the "The Royal Seed", for had Joash been murdered, the line of Judah would have been finished. The royal line of our Lord!

My Purpose as a Woman

There are many small mentions of faithful women in the Bible.

> *"A little maid told her mistress that a man of God could heal Naaman of his leprosy"* (2 Kgs. 5:2,3).

A widow's mite surpassed all the rich gifts given by rich people in the temple (Luke 21:3). Your attitude could be "I am just a woman", but would you not like to be thought of as "a just woman."

> *"The just shall live by faith"* (Rom. 1:17).

O My Soul
A Biblical Exploration of Soul-talk
By Marilyn F. McClurg

Why I wrote *O My Soul*: I had struggled for some time to learn to bring my thoughts into captivity to Jesus Christ, as we are admonished in 2 Corinthians 10:5. It became apparent in my study of God's Word that those who managed to so discipline their minds talked, not to themselves, but to their immortal soul. Over a period of four or five years, I collected an astounding list of Bible passages about soul-talk and began to understand that when my soul is blessing God, I cannot be complaining, worrying, or arguing. However, I cannot bless the Lord until I cast down thoughts that exalt themselves against the knowledge of God. After I rebuke those wicked ideas, I can talk to my soul in biblical phrases somewhat like praying the words of Scripture back to God. I felt compelled to share the results of this spiritual journey with others who struggle in their thought life as I have.

ISBN: 9781926765310
Canadian $10.99
US $9.99

I WILL PUBLISH THE NAME OF THE LORD
GOSPEL FOLIO PRESS
www.gospelfolio.com • 1-800-952-2382

CPSIA information can be obtained at www.ICGtesting.com
Printed in the USA
LVOW041130041211

257722LV00006B/2/P